# THE PERFECT SPECULATOR

## HOW TO WIN BIG IN UP MARKETS AND LOSE NOTHING IN DOWN MARKETS

# THE PERFECT SPECULATOR

## HOW TO WIN BIG IN UP MARKETS AND LOSE NOTHING IN DOWN MARKETS

### BRAD KOTESHWAR

The Perfect Speculator

Great Expressions Publishing
34522 North Scottsdale Road #254
Scotttsdale, AZ 85262

All the characters in this book are fictional. Any resemblance of the
characters to any one living or dead is by accident and purely coincidental.
The events in the book may or may not have occurred and may or may not
be fictional. If the events have occurred in the past, they might or might
not have been used as an example to offer the market's lessons. If the
events have not occurred yet, they may or may not occur in the future.

Book Design and Layout by
www.integrativeink.com

ISBN 0-9769324-0-7

PRINTED IN THE UNITED STATES OF AMERICA

To my daughter,
who like the markets,
has taught me much

The speculator observes, interprets and then
executes based on best-odds of making profits

# TABLE OF CONTENTS

# PREFACE

I was at the corner barber shop getting a hair-cut. I liked old-fashioned barber shops. Nowadays, glorified barber shops were sprouting all over. With names that were hard to pronounce and the word "Salon" next to them, the modern-day barbers calling themselves "hairstylists," were taking free license to charge three times what a standard barber-shop hair-cut should cost. My best guess was that my barber, Ed, was in his late seventies. As he was cutting my hair, he was talking about his younger days when he ran a barber shop just outside of Chicago. I asked him, "When did you move to Arizona?" He said he had retired about ten years ago and had moved to Arizona right after he had sold his barber shop in Chicago. Then the obvious question popped in to my mind which I blurted out quite tactlessly, "Why are you still working if you had retired ten years ago?" He said with a tinge of sadness and with some anger in his voice, "I should have listened to folks like you. But I had my money in mutual funds and the bear market wiped me out. Here I am in my golden years at the worst financial condition I have ever been."

As I was driving home after my hair-cut, I made a mental note to myself that the media never talks about the thousands and thousands of stories that are similar to or worse than Ed's. The hype in the market place is always about the large promise of quick riches that the stock market offers.

It was a beautiful spring morning in early April in Scottsdale. I was basking in my fifteen minutes of fame as Time magazine had just mentioned me and my wife in one of their business columns. Time magazine had covered the phenomenal price run-up and the subsequent price collapse of Taser International's stock. In that article they had mentioned a little something about me.

I had written a book in 2004 titled, "The Perfect Stock," which was based on Taser's great price run. My phone was ringing off the hook as family, friends and even my neighbors were calling me saying that I was the only one they ever knew personally who had made it into Time magazine. I had to remind most folks that a new issue of Time was already on the stands and last week's Time magazine was now ancient history. Human memory being short, Taser was a forgotten story. No doubt that future market cycles would bring along with them many more new stocks that would write similar stories like that of Taser.

Among the many calls I got were a few from the big New York book publishing houses. Now that my name had made it into Time magazine, apparently they had picked up my earlier book, which I had self-published back in September of 2004. These big boys did not mince words. They came straight to the point. "How many copies of your first book have you sold? How has the Time magazine article jump-started the sales? Do you have any other books that you are working on right now? Have you been approached by any other publisher? Can you send us a rough manuscript of your second book, if you have one?" The questions all seemed to be the same.

I did not know how they figured out that I was working on my second book. But I was flattered by all the attention I was getting. I was more than happy to send them all a draft copy of my manuscript I had developed by then.

A week or so later I got a call from one of the publishers. This fellow was blunt and to the point. He said, "Brad, your manuscript is great but I am sorry I cannot sell it. You cover the classic principles in a very simple and conversational style. I think the readers will enjoy it and learn from it. However, I cannot see anything in the book that promises easy riches and there is nothing in the book that I can use as a new-get-rich-quick method to create a marketing buzz around. I do not see a new and easy way to beat the market in the book."

I interrupted him and said, "David, I hate to say it but there is no quick-and-easy get-rich quick method in the market. If one existed, it would have been devised by now. Speculation has been around for thousands of years. Nothing has changed. I have put down the lessons in a very simple and easy reading format. I would have loved to have had a book like this when I was a youngster. I would have avoided huge mistakes I have made along the way."

David was abrupt. He replied, "I cannot hype your new manuscript and nor can I sell it. When I push a book on the market, it is usually a new way to get rich quickly in the market. The public is always looking for short-cuts and loves to pay big bucks for a fancy new way to beat the market. If I hype it and market it, I can sell thousands of copies on Day One. Do you know Jill Incognito? When she writes a book, no matter how bad, she sells 20,000 books on Day One. I can hype it, sell it, push it, market it. Her books always offer a way to get rich quick and the public buys her message without blinking."

"It is an inside joke in the publishing world - we only publish books that usually do not need any help in selling. If you change your mind and come up with a book that touts a new cutting-edge way to beat the market, let me know and I will hype it, buzz it, push it and make it a best-seller. The public is funny that way as they will pay to read a pie-in-the-sky promise any day but will never pay to learn the true lessons of the market."

"The true market lessons and the realities of the markets are too hard to implement because the public wants easy money. Easy money does not exist. The only easy money is in selling promises of easy money. Just ask Jill. Do you know who I am talking about?" I knew Jill. She was a perennial bull. She only knew two kinds of markets - a bull market and a super-bull market. She was always claiming to be right. The public, however, did not mind that Jill was always pointing out wins only in hindsight. It only mattered to the public that Jill was an optimist and according to Jill a great big bull market was always just around the corner.

I commented that this Jill, David was talking about, had a great gig going. She would publish in her newspaper all the stocks that had already made a serious move over the most recent few months. She would then add a comment which would say, "If you had bought this stock six months ago, you could have tripled your money. To find stocks like this, you should subscribe to my charting service and my screening programs." Obviously, the charts and the screens would cost a pretty penny.

When any of her readers would raise a valid and a smart question, "Why is that your paper does not offer the stocks as potential buys before the move starts but you always indicate after-the-fact which stocks have made a move?" - her reply would be a classic salesman's disarming answer, "We are a newspaper and not an investment advisor. We offer tools for the investor to make great returns."

I went on with my thoughts, "I find such an approach disingenuous and nothing more than peddling false promises of riches. But then, the stock market's job is to seduce the naïve with such lures of quick riches." I was being harsh but I figured David was an insider in the publishing business and was used to candid comments from his potential authors.

David abruptly interrupted me and said, "But Brad, that is exactly what the public hungers for. It is unbelievable to most people, but people will buy a get-rich-quick scheme any day over a true and accurate portrayal of the reality of the markets. Reality is too hard to accept. People want to believe that huge amounts of gains can be made easily in the markets. They will pay big bucks to be sold into the idea that any one can easily make big bucks in the markets. They will keep coming back for more if you keep churning out such books and services."

"The market is demand driven. Where there is a demand, we offer the supply. The demand is in get-rich-quick short-cuts and promises of easy money. More people lose money in the markets than anyone will admit. These losers all want to make back their money quickly and easily. That is what we offer - a promise of easy money. And selling books and services to capture that demand is easy money for us."

I knew this to be the truth. Not only through my own experiences as a broker in the commodities market, but also from the experiences of others in the business. It is frustrating when you offer a rare service that can pin-point the right steps to avoid the pot-holes and make use of the right opportunities, but nobody will buy in because the work is taxing, hard, requires a lot of patience, persistence and takes a special mental make-up to get the hang of things.

David went on, "Another drawback with your work is that you do not use any well-known CNBC types or Wall Street types in your book. If you interview some well-known folks, you will find that selling the book is easy. The public is celebrity driven. Any celebrity or well-known individual will help propel the sales of a book."

I said to David, "That is okay, David. I will pursue the book by self-publishing it. This way I will have complete independence on what I write, how I write and when I write. You are correct. Your form of publishing seems to me a lot like the way the insiders act on Wall Street. It is mainly hype and produced to create and fill a demand. Nothing wrong with that form of capitalism. It just is not my style."

David was cold in his response and said, "Good luck. No leading media outlet ever reviews self-published work. In addition, you will have a hard time marketing the book since most traditional big New York publishers have an in-road into all the radio, TV and print interview and coverage for their own authors. A self-published writer has absolutely no chance of getting any kind of exposure."

"In addition, a self-published title has no chance of making it into the leading bookstores and chain stores like Wal-mart, Barnes & Noble, Borders, B. Dalton and the like. It is folks like us, the big traditional publishers, who have the ability and the contractual arrangements to place our books on the bookshelves of book stores. In addition, with our in-house employees numbering in the thousands, we can make our own hundreds of reviews on all the leading online retailers like Amazon. A self-publisher like you has no such machinery in place to push your books. I am afraid you will not be able to profit much with your book sales. Moreover, what do you know about filling it up? We publishers know a little something about filling up a book with many many pages of redundant and useless information. We can fill up pages and pages of stuff just to make the book look fat and full of information. We added an index, a glossary, etc. just to make more pages within a book. As you know more the number of pages, higher the price we can charge."

David was right in all respects. Though America offered more opportunities than any other nation, it still was operating within a good old boys' network. No matter how good a book is, getting the exposure to the media and the public at large was a key factor in making a book a best-seller. If the public is not made aware of a good book, there is little chance of the book being bought or read when there are hundreds of thousands of new books coming out every year, vast majority of which are peddled, pushed, hyped, marketed, and sold by the big boys.

There was nothing surprising in David's comments. I was an old hand at the markets and getting older by the minute. I have been around this game long enough to know the realities. I was not looking to make riches off my book. I wanted to leave behind a little something that I had learned by myself and also through the lessons offered to me by one of the greatest speculators of modern times, Boyd Hunt. Boyd was unknown to the rest of the world and he preferred to keep it that way. I was fortunate enough to know Boyd well and some of his operations in the market were downright unbelievable.

The information about and the rules of successful speculation are in this book. Just how one can accept, interpret and implement the rules of the game is up to each player.

# Chapter 1
## The Speculator's Call

Boyd Hunt was a masterful speculator. I knew some very successful speculators but Boyd was by far the best and in a league of his own. He was now in his nineties and was more reclusive than he was a few years back. But then he was always very discreet and unassuming. One could have had an hour's chat with Boyd without knowing that he was a very successful market operator. What he knew about the markets was worth millions if used correctly.

It was in early 2005 that I received a call from him. It had been some months since my report about Taser's phenomenal price run of 7000% in 52 weeks had been written. As it happened, the report somehow got out to the local media and in order to quell the furor that might have erupted, I had published the report in the form of a fiction and made it available to the public at large. That book was titled, "The Perfect Stock." And as it turned out, the book had been received reasonably well, especially for an unknown first time author who had self-published the work. But it had been of some disappointment that some readers could not grasp the lessons that were buried in that book. I figured it had been due to my own shortcomings as a writer. I was not an expert on the English language. And my mind was focused more on incorporating the market lessons within the fiction rather than trying to be politically and otherwise correct with impeccable use of written English.

Once the report was released as a fictional account, in order to protect certain identities and events, the media somehow seemed to lose interest. It became clear to me later that most of the local media owned Taser stocks. And no one wanted to hear

1

in the fall of 2004 that the stock had topped out in April 2004. As it turned out, the April 2004 top was about as close to the top as it got. In 2005 alone, Taser had fallen from a high of $33 down to a $7-$10 price range by the time spring rolled around. I was not about to go around town claiming, "I told you so." That was not my style and Taser was now an old story anyway. In addition, I had been wrong many times in the market as well. Though, through the years I had learned to be wrong small and right big.

When Boyd called me, I was a little anxious. What did he want from me? Did he find my use of his character in my first book upsetting? I had used some of his trading records and techniques in my book while attempting to show the actions of a great speculator. It had been months since I had spoken to him last. I had kept my word and I had taken great precautions to protect his identity as he was indeed a very private person. I had used a fictional name instead of his real name and I had attached a fictional location for his home. Was he calling now to inform me that he was not happy with the references I had made to his trades which resembled so closely to his actual executions on Taser's stock?

It was an early morning in January of 2005. It was a little after 6:00 a.m. As is my daily routine, I was drinking black coffee and reading the business sections of The New York Times and of The Arizona Republic. The phone rang. I answered. It was Boyd. He asked me to drive up to meet him for breakfast as soon as possible. He said that he had something very important to discuss with me and he needed my presence immediately. I sensed the urgency and agreed to drive up the hill to meet him right away.

As I pulled up his driveway, I was deep in thought and somewhat curious about the reason for Boyd's call. But I still managed to appreciate the beautiful view of the valley below in the early morning bright but crisp Arizona winter sun. Boyd was sitting pool side sipping his coffee. He stood up to shake my hand. I noticed he looked older and he sounded tired as he wished me good morning.

He handed me a fresh cup of coffee and said, "Thank you for coming on such a short notice. But I am working on borrowed time. During my last physical my doctor found some tumors in my lungs and I am afraid I have lung cancer."

I was shocked. I had never seen him smoke. All I could say was, "How can that be? You are not a smoker. I am sorry, Boyd. But I do not know what to say. This is terrible."

He waved his hand and said that he had been a heavy smoker for many many years in his younger days. He had quit in his fifties. But the damage done to his lungs in his younger days had apparently caught up with him. He was not much interested in talking about his illness. He came directly to the point and said, "As you know I have a handful of old friends for whom I write a small stock market commentary. They have asked me that I find someone to take over my commentary. I could not think of anyone else. Your name was the first and the only name that came to my mind."

I was thrown off-guard. This was totally out of the blue and unexpected. First, I was still stunned by the news of Boyd's failing health. On top of that, he now placed this new heavy burden on me. I was dumbfounded and I just sat there staring at him. I opened my mouth but words would not come out. Boyd saw my discomfort, smiled and said in his usual cool and calm voice, "Do not worry. I am sure it will not interfere with your time and other obligations as I know for a fact that you already do most of what I do in order to get the market's read. And I also know that based on your read of the market, you pick potential stock winners as well. That is pretty much what I offer to my readers. And I still have some time to help you through the basics and allow you to get comfortable with writing your own interpretation of the market's moods."

I gathered myself and took a deep breath and replied, "I am indeed flattered, Boyd. But I am afraid my knowledge about the markets is not nearly as great as yours. In addition, I can think of at least one or two other fellows in the valley who can do a better job than I can."

"Don't sell yourself short. I know who you are talking about but they are tied down to other interests. And they are tied into the Wall Street machinery and that makes it impossible for them to be unbiased and independent. I need somebody totally removed from the influences of the insiders. It has to be someone with no attachment to anyone who could be an insider at any given moment. I need someone who is and can be detached completely from the Wall Street machinery. I am sorry to say that you are about the only one I can think of at the moment," said Boyd.

I replied, "Even if I fit the bill, I must admit my ability to read the market and individual stocks is limited. I do not have the kind of experience in the markets as you do. Nor do I have the insight, the feel and the ability to cut through the noise that you do. You have learned your craft over decades of experience and successful market operations. I would come short, way short, in meeting the needs of your readers."

While we were exchanging our views, Boyd was busy bringing in boxes from his study out to the pool side. Without realizing, I was following him in and out of his house while helping him carry box after box out on to the pool deck. Before I realized it, we had stacked more than a handful of boxes out on the deck. I noticed the boxes were numbered and were full of papers. By now my voice was slowly trailing off as it appeared that Boyd was not listening to me. He would open each box, glance quickly at the papers at the top of the box and then move on to the next box. Once he had given such a quick glance at each of the boxes, he settled down and sat back.

"Do these boxes bring back memories?" I asked. Boyd nodded and said, "Yes. There is an invaluable amount of knowledge here. If I had known what I know now when I began in the 1930s, I could have done an incredible amount of good." It was not like he had not done enough good. But like all humans, there is the thinking that things could have been better if some of the lessons learned had been learned earlier and quicker.

I was getting very nervous. It didn't seem that he was going to change his mind. He was bent on me taking over his work. I felt inadequate. I knew I was gifted with a quick mind. But he was an operator whose mind worked at a much higher plane. He seemed to sense my hesitancy and he said, "I saw your report on the Taser operation. I appreciated your candid appraisal of that stock as well as the market's workings. It is common for the public to be lulled into misplaced confidence that using technical, mathematical models and other cerebral sounding methods, a superior set of returns are available."

"Your writings were simple and expressed honestly. I need someone who can offer similar simple, direct and honest interpretation of the market without any threat of retribution from the insiders. Anybody can and everybody does offer a bullish scenario to get the public excited. A clear bullish scenario only comes about 30-40% of the time. In a ten-year cycle a clean bullish condition comes about three or four times. I am focused on being that rare person who can make big money during such bullish conditions and at the same time can stay in safe modes and not lose anything during the balance of the time. Almost everybody has made money in the markets at some time or another. That is what keeps us coming back to the market time and again. But very few have been able to keep what they made. The market usually takes it all and more back. It takes some gumption to interpret and state it plainly that not every rally is the beginning of a bull trend. And similarly, not every sell-off is the beginning of a bear trend."

I had the feeling that he had me then. I was always skeptical of the hype and the media's take about the market. And I had been through more than a few market cycles to know that the ability of the market to fool most folks was great. And the probability of humans being right in the market was low. Boyd confirmed his approach was not that much different than mine. He said, "I always approached the market with an acceptance that I was dealing with a tricky and a dangerous entity. I preferred to come into the market with a clear focus on the probability of wins."

"I am a simple man. I like a simple life. I try to simplify everything as I hate confusion. And as soon as something starts getting complicated, I get thoroughly confused. So I have learned the importance of keeping things simple. I cannot operate in any other way. I have no understanding of the latest mathematical models, software, probability models, econometrics, etc. I figure if that is what it takes to be successful as a speculator, why is that I do not see tons of mathematicians who are great speculators? And why are the cutting edge mathematicians being hired by brokerages and research entities to develop and maintain tons and tons of mathematical models? I mean, if the math models were so great, why are the great math minds working for brokerages in research and model building instead of successfully trading in the markets? I think it is such a classic human tendency not to be left behind that when one brokerage loads up with scientists and math geniuses in its research department, other brokerages follow suit so that they are not left behind in the quest for the magic answer in beating the market."

"There are no infallible systems. If there was one, the market would cease to exist. As the infallible system will clean up the market. Once one accepts that fact, one is well on his or her way to getting a grip on the market. As long as one is still looking for that infallible system, he or she will continue to be beaten up by the market. And the second point of reality one needs to face is that all that is needed to be a successful speculator is in the price/volume action of leading stocks and leading indices."

"I have found that there are offers of all kinds of cutting edge market-beating signals and methods to snare up the gullible public. Everyone claims to have found the magic answer to beat the market. There is no such thing as a sure thing. And the market in its genius way sets us all up by offering crumbs once in a while so that we keep coming back for more. Every trading system works for some small duration of time at some point in a market cycle. That is just enough rope offered to the gullible public to hang themselves. Of course, nobody wants to hear this because then they have to accept that they cannot find a short-cut to riches. And who doesn't want a short-cut to riches?"

"My approach is very simple. As I said, I am a simple man. I keep my operations very simple. If something is not coming out and staring at me straight in the face, then in all likelihood it is the market trying to trap me with temptations. More money has been lost in trying to make small incremental amounts of gains than people will ever realize. The common man on the street has no chance of outdoing the research done by the biggest brokerages, researchers, fund managers, investment bankers, etc. These entities have the best and the brightest working for them. They do some of the best research."

"I cannot do a superior research than these big boys. But I can see what the big boys do with the research in the way they buy and sell stocks. I see it plainly on the index and individual stock's price and volume action. That to me is all the information that is needed. I just follow the big money. But to get to that point, I spent years learning. It is only the large gains I have made that has confirmed what all top speculators know. It is all in the price and volume action. And the rest of the stuff in the market is pure fluff."

I interjected by saying, "Boyd, I agree with you. But how did you manage to convince your readers that price/volume action is all there is to know? I find that when I simplify matters, the public cannot believe that it could be that simple. They want to believe in a jargon filled techno-mumbo-jumbo from an unproven service that relies on hype and flash, rather than a simple straight forward and an honest appraisal of the market."

To which he replied, "Yes. We humans want to believe that the secret to market success is something deep and complicated. The reasoning is quite simple. It is so hard to be successful that it must be complicated. It cannot be simple. So, anyone who can sound complicated, show a lot of flash and color, use some long words and some complicated mathematics is immediately thought to be a genius in the markets. But my readers know better because they are no spring chickens either. They have in their day spent millions on top notch researchers and cutting edge models and lost even more, especially during bear runs. They have learned the hard way my first and true lesson, which is, first, - do no harm. It takes a genius to understand and recognize that not losing is actually winning. Hardly anybody recognizes this. And consequently, you hardly see any consistently successful speculators in the markets. They are there but very few and far between because most of the people never understand the concept of avoiding losses."

I asked him then about a commonly held view that one needs to pay a great deal of attention to earnings growth. I knew exactly what he would say since he boiled everything down to the basics, but I asked Boyd anyway, "Do you eliminate stocks which do not show earnings growth? After all, the internet bubble taught folks that lack of earnings was the downfall of many dotcom stocks that went bust."

He smiled a knowing smile and replied, "You know that it is the anticipation of earnings that is more important than actual earnings. Earnings growth is in many cases a lagging indicator. Many times a big move has already occurred and gone before a young company can show actual earnings. The stock market is forward looking. The move happens in anticipation of. Not because of. It is common for the novices and amateurs to focus solely on earnings growth. That is what the insiders want the public to focus on. After all, the insiders cannot sell their holdings unless there is a big pool of buyers for the insiders' holdings."

"Usually, by the time earnings growth has been firmly established, the better part of a stock's move has already gone by. It goes back to my earlier discussion about the research that the big boys do. Remember, they have an army of researchers who have already forecasted and anticipated all that needs to be anticipated. The big money places its position based on what is anticipated down the road. Not because what earnings were for the quarters gone by. In an environment where everything is discounted based on anticipated conditions and events months in advance, what good is earnings of quarters gone by and already in the past. Today's news is ancient history. The news is used to shakeout and fake-out the amateurs. In the longer term, news only acts as a lagging confirmation of the move of a stock that has occurred weeks or months ago. I pay attention to anticipation of earnings. Not actual earnings history. As I said, even today's news is ancient history in the market."

"It is obvious to my readers, who possess a great deal of common sense, that it would be foolhardy to think that the common man can out do in research what the big behemoths do And by extension, since these big moneyed folks place large funds into the stocks they like, all I need to do is follow the big money and I would thus follow the best research in the country. There cannot be a simpler method to function well in the market than this. Follow the big money's price/volume action to see what the big boys are doing. The price/volume action shows to me where big money is buying, where they are selling and where they are supporting a stock."

"But these big boys know that folks like us will follow their money. So they will offer red herrings and many times create fake-outs and shake-outs to throw us off our game. This is because they have smart minds paying attention to the price/volume action on their holdings as well. So they see the same things I see. This is where sound money management comes into play. And at the same time looking for confirming signs becomes crucial. This is where staying out of the market is just as important as getting in. There will be periods where nothing looks good from a price/volume perspective. And even if something looks good, market conditions make it impossible to be successful as the market does not offer decent odds of winning. In such periods, it is very important not be active in the market. It is very important to sit back and wait and observe the market action. This is very very hard for most folks. There is always someone hyping some stock all the time. To sit back and not fall for the hype is extremely hard for most folks."

"I am hoping that you will take my offer and help me out by taking up my work. My readers are savvy and well experienced. And they are just a few of them. I am not looking for more readers. These are the few clients who have been with me for years and years. I do this to appreciate their loyalty to and confidence in me. They are not looking for guidance. But are only looking for an independent view of the markets. They just wish to see if what you see is what they see. They are looking for confirmation. I have full confidence in your abilities. I will be happy to spend the next few days with you and cover some of the basics of the market for you if you wish. But if you feel uncomfortable in listening to what I have to say, I can just let you have these boxes. I am sure some of the cycles I have recorded in these boxes will come back in the future in some form or another. And the notes I have included may be of some help. If you decide to take up my offer, we will need to start getting together rather urgently."

Boyd could be very persuasive in his quiet low key fashion. I was still unsure about my abilities to write my thoughts about the market. I had my good years and my bad years like everyone else.

But my good years had never been as good as Boyd's good years. And worse still, my bad years were always worse than Boyd's worst years. And though my report on Taser had become public by now, I knew my writing style was not the greatest. I had the tendency to write as I thought. In short, succinct and crisp sentences. And for some folks getting the hang of what seemed disjointed was harder than I had envisioned.

I explained this shortcoming of my writing style to Boyd. I was an old dog. And if I had not developed a great writing style by now, I surely was not going to learn to do it now when I was in my forties. I did not want his readers to be disappointed when they saw a different style of writing, especially since they had become used to Boyd's elegant writing.

Boyd replied, "Do not worry about that. You are not writing a work of literature. Nobody expects you to. What my readers expect is a knowledgeable, sincere, honest, straight-forward and, most of all, independently unbiased interpretation of the market's action. They are looking for a constant drum-beat reiterating sound principles of successful speculation. We are like children in that regard. We need a constant drum-beat of never ending repetition of sound speculation principles. Human memory is short. If not repeated often enough, we forget. If my readers really want literature, I am sure there are plenty of great works freely available to them on the market. Nobody is looking for an award winning writing. What is needed is repetitive rules of losing small in bad markets and winning big in good markets."

Seeing my hesitation, he continued, "Why don't you sleep on the idea. Take these boxes home with you. Go over the notes you will find in these boxes. Take the weekend to consider all the angles. Talk it over with your lovely wife and then make your decision. If you decide to pursue this, I would like to spend a few hours with you brushing up on some simple lessons of the markets. I think it will help you in sticking to first principles of speculation which is what my readers rely heavily on."

It was then I realized that Boyd's insight and lessons would offer me the simple genius of a successful speculator. I asked him even if I did not accept the work, would he be kind enough to spend the next few days and let me in on some of his market operations. What I knew was nothing compared what he knew about the markets. He nodded his acceptance.

After a few minutes of discussions about his health and the bleak prognosis, he stood up to let me know that he was done with me for the morning. We shook hands. It was mid-morning and I headed back home. My car was full of Boyd's boxes.

I drove back home deep in thought. This was heavy. It was a lot for me to handle for one morning. I pulled up to my garage and started hauling the boxes one by one into my office. I had a small but efficient office at home. Once I unloaded the boxes, the office suddenly started to look like an overstuffed closet.

I spent the weekend going over some of the best years and some of the worst years in terms of the gains made by the S&P 500 index over the recent past. I downloaded the data for the S&P500 from the internet. I picked out the corresponding years' records from Boyd's boxes. I made some notes. I noticed with great interest that during the best years shown by the S&P 500, Boyd had made a killing in the market. And during the absolute worst years, Boyd had not traded at all and had not lost anything.

That Sunday night I went into a detailed conversation with my wife about Boyd, his poor health and his proposal. I needed an objective, intelligent and an intuitive feedback from someone I trusted and from someone who knew me well.

It was past midnight, well past my bed-time. I had arrived at my decision. I walked into my office and sent an email to Boyd and accepted his offer to take up writing his commentary. I knew he checked his emails first thing in the morning. It was too late in the night to call him. I figured he wanted an answer from me at the earliest, so an email was the best way to communicate with him.

I had learned long ago that empty vessels make a lot of noise. In the market place, the braggarts and the chest-thumpers are usually not the successful ones. The truly successful ones are the silent and anonymous types. And Boyd was among the most successful, anonymous and silent operators around.

I knew I was going to learn much about successful speculation from an expert. It was going to be up to me to make good use of the information. The tools would be available to me at my fingertips. How I would discipline myself and use the rules of speculation would determine my success in the market. But I needed to keep myself focused to achieve the results. Being focused and avoiding being side-tracked was going to be the biggest challenge.

## **Summary:**

The average retail speculator has no chance of out-researching the vast machinery on the Street. The Street has some of best, the brightest, the most educated, the most trained, the most intelligent and the most experienced folks working. Therefore, the best way to be on the "inside" with the most knowledgeable folks is to follow their action. They take action based on all the exhaustive research that they conduct. And such action shows up clearly to the diligent and patient market operator through the price and volume action on the leading indices in conjunction with the price and volume action on leading stocks. Once one learns to decipher the price and volume action, one has started on the path of successful speculation.

# CHAPTER 2
## CAN SPECULATION BE LEARNED?

The following morning as I was reading the morning papers, I received a call from Boyd. He thanked me for accepting his offer. He wanted to begin work on moving things along immediately. His time was limited and he was not taking any chances. He wanted me to meet him yet again for breakfast. He made the breakfast meeting a daily thing for the following few days. It was during these breakfast meetings that I was given the gift of knowledge from one of the most successful speculators of my time. And like most extremely successful speculators, Boyd was an artist. He had mastered the true art of speculation.

One of the first questions that morning I asked Boyd was whether speculation can be learned. He replied that it can be learned and should be learned by anyone who ventures into the markets. Without specific and firm rules of speculation, humans are doomed to fail in their quest for riches in the financial markets. I asked him how he had learned the art of speculation because I know speculation is an art and not a science. And I asked him to explain how speculation, the art, is confused by novices as science. Boyd said, "Science relies on proven facts and theorems before arriving at a definitive conclusion. Speculation relies on observation first and then executing or acting based on the observed events with only regard to probability of the outcome. And each subsequent action is based on the outcome of the previous action. And nothing is conclusive in the art of speculation. It took me years of experience and learning through losses to understand that speculation is an art."

I asked him to expound on this a little bit because I was not very clear on what he was saying. So he said, "Let us take science, for example. Newton observed that the apple fell down from the tree. He then observed and noted all objects fall down toward the earth when thrown upward in the air. After confirming that everything comes back to earth, he concluded that earth has a gravitational pull and physical objects will come back to earth. He concluded with scientific certainty that earth has a gravitational pull. That is science. Nobody can argue against that."

"Speculation, on the other hand, is an art. There is no certainty in speculation. In fact, there is absolute uncertainty in speculation and absolute uncertainty is the only certainty to a successful speculator. As a result, there is no way it can be a science. If it were a science, we should have a great level of certainty in its outcome. We know that is not the case. Just take any report card of all the professionals in the market place and you will note that only 10-15% of participants will outperform the market averages in any randomly chosen year. Which means 85% of the people will be beaten by the market in any given year. 85% chance of the market beating the speculator proves that successful speculation is not a science but an art."

"If one insists on speculation being a scientific process, then one has lost even before entering the market. It is the human mind that will be the culprit in killing most trading accounts. To be successful in speculation, the first and foremost act is to face the fact that it is an art. If one is looking for scientific rules and results, one should stick to academics and to doing research. A scientist should never execute a trade because execution of a trade offers only one of two outcomes. A winning trade or a losing trade. And with 85% of the trades placed in the market place having a return less than the market average, probabilities of a winning trade placed on pure science are very low. A scientist should be able to appreciate probabilities more than most and with odds like these, he would never make a trade."

"The biggest drawback with a scientific approach to the market is that it has no protection if one is wrong. A scientific approach inherently has a certainty in its outcome. As a result, a scientist will place a trade and will not have an offset in the case that the trade turns out to be wrong and leads to a loss. In other words, since a scientist is certain of the trade's outcome, he will never place an offsetting trade to liquidate the position if the trade starts to lose."

"A speculator or the artist, will allow for the fact that he could be wrong. And if he is wrong, he needs to eliminate the loss taking position promptly and look for a subsequent trade to place the right trade. A speculator first observes the market and individual stocks to see if a confirmed trend is visible. Until he can observe a confirmed trend, he will not place a trade."

I interrupted Boyd and asked him to explain what he meant by a confirmed trend. I could recognize a trend when I saw one. But Boyd had a way of explaining things that made the complex look simple. I, on the other hand, had trouble with words. And he proved how at ease he was in explaining matters about the market by saying, "A trend is something that is moving in one direction clearly. An up trend is a market that is moving up. A down trend is a market that is moving down. But markets do not move up or down in a straight line. However, in a confirmed up trend, the market moves up a little and then reacts and moves down a little. But the move down or the reaction is less than the first move up. Then it moves up yet again. This time it moves up to a point much higher than the high it made the previous time it moved up. Then it reacts and moves down again. But the down move reaches down to point that is much higher than the lowest point during the last down move. In essence, we are seeing a series of higher highs and higher lows. This a confirmed up trend. A down trend works in exact reverse. A confirmed down trend is when a series of lower highs and lower lows are being pegged by the market or the stock."

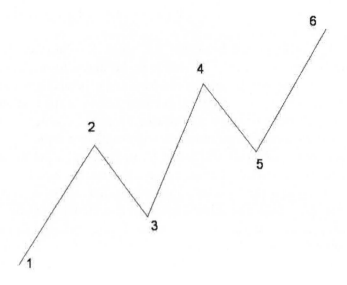

**Figure 1. A confirmed up trend**

1 = most recent low

2 = a near term high pegged by an up trending stock

3 = a reactionary low pegged in response to the high pegged at point 2

4 = new higher high above the prior high of point 2

5 = a reactionary low to the most recent high at point 4

6 = a new higher high

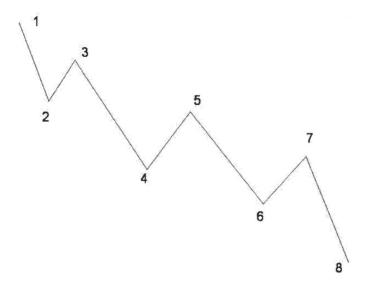

**Figure 2. A confirmed down trend**

1 = most recent high

2 = a near term term low is pegged by a down trending stock

3 = a reactionary high is pegged in response to the downward leg from point 1 to point 2

4 = a new lower low is pegged in continuation of the down trend

5 = a reactionary high is lower than the prior high at point 3

6 = a new lower low is pegged

7 = the reactionary high is yet again lower than the prior high at point 5

8 = continuation of the down trend

"The average Joe who comes into the market does not even know who he is. He has no clue if he is a trader, an investor, a gambler or a speculator. In all likelihood, he has not ever spent a second to figure out what his own personality is. He has not spent any time to understand how he will approach the market and its traps. Is he a gambler? A gambler will act without any regard to odds of wins. Is he an investor? An investor, by definition, is someone who looks for a guaranteed rate of return on his investments. Since the stock market does not offer guaranteed rate of returns, an investor has no place in the stock market. Is he a trader? If he is a trader, then he must be the kind who gets in for a few scalper's points and gets out. Again, with odds being against anyone batting higher than .500, a trader has no chance of winning year after year, cycle after cycle. But is it not amazing that the Wall Street machinery always talks in terms of investors and traders. I have never heard the Street talk about appealing to the speculators. That is because everybody knows that the speculator will place his commitments only when odds favor him. Such an approach cannot be encouraged by the insiders as that will not help them unload their shares to willing buyers at the right time."

Boyd continued, "A speculator will not make commitments until he has clearly seen at least one set of higher highs to confirm an up trend or one set of lower lows to confirm a down trend. I call it a zig or a zag. I need to see at least one zig or one zag to prove the beginning of a trend. And once I see a zig or a zag, we come to the first step. Which is exactly what the speculator has now observed. Now the second step is to time his first trade. Not only does he need to time his trade, but he must also manage his money so that should he be wrong in his interpretation based on his observation, he will lose small amounts. At this early point, the speculator is not looking to make a killing. He is just trying to confirm if he is in sync with the market. So he starts using his money management techniques. I will talk more about money management in the coming days."

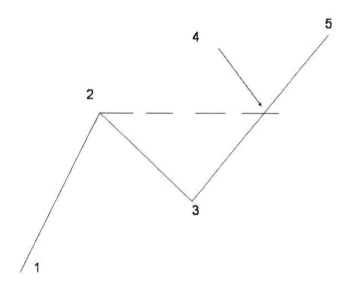

**Figure 3. A zig showing a potential up trend**

1 = prior up trend

2 = most recent high

3 = reactionary low to the most recent high

4 = as the high point pegged at point 2 is overcome and cleared, a potential new up trend may have begun

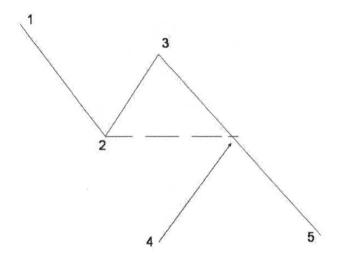

**Figure 4. A zag showing a potential down trend**

1 = prior down trend

2 = most recent low

3 = reactionary high to the most recent low

4 = as the new low point pegged at point 2 is penetrated to the down side, a potential new down trend may have begun

"I think the one thing I wish you to take away from today's chat is that a speculator will first observe the market's and the stock's action. After observation, he will interpret what he observed. And once he interprets the market and the stock action, he will execute a trade. But he will always execute his trades with the protection against losses and an acceptance that the interpretation could be wrong. He will not execute his second trade until his first trade proves to him that his interpretation was correct. From then on, each subsequent action is completely based on the outcome of the previous move. Yes, there is a degree of subjectivity that comes about in what the speculator interprets.

As I said, it is an art and not a science. Once he interprets the market's and the stock's action, he then places a trade. As if you did not know, the word 'speculation' comes from the Latin root 'speculari', which means to observe or to spy. Observation and interpretation of the observed movements are the first steps. We will cover everything step by step. But for today, I have to stop here as I feel a little tired."

And with that he stood up to leave. To illustrate the point about up trends and down trends and the zigs and the zags, he had drawn a few lines on a sheet of paper subconsciously. I picked up the sheet of paper with his illustrations and placed it on my legal pad. I wanted to see the market operations from Boyd's point of view. So I was very careful to make notes in great detail.

## Summary:

Speculation is an art. Speculation involves three steps. Observation, interpretation and action. The speculator first observes the market and the leading stocks for clues. Then he interprets his observed events. Once his interpretation leads him to believe that the odds of winning are at least equal or better than the odds of losing, he then takes action. A speculator will always look for signals from the market and not from humans. A successful speculator places his actions based on probabilities and his second step is based on the success of the first step. And the third step is based on the success of the second step. And so on.

# CHAPTER 3
## FIRST, DO NO HARM

Buried within the Hippocratic oath's modern version is a line which says, "I will prevent disease whenever I can, for prevention is preferable to cure."

There cannot be a better way to explain the rule of "first, do no harm." Boyd calls it his mantra. That morning he was more upbeat. It was yet another glorious Arizona winter morning. And his cheerfulness seemed to rub off on me as I was smiling ear to ear throughout that morning's lessons.

Before going any further with our discussions that morning, Boyd said that he wished to make a disclaimer. He said, "What I discuss here is something that has worked for me. I cannot say it will work for everybody. This is the only method that I have found which works for me. My method is a lot like free democracy. It is a lousy system. But it surely beats all other systems I have seen and tried. The beauty of my form of trading is that it keeps me out of trouble in bad markets and lets me have the best chance of winning big in good markets. And I have boiled it down to a systematic approach where I am not asked to try to be cerebral and intellectual. I am not asked to decipher complicated formula or methods. Everything is kept simple for the sole reason that I am a simple man. I hate complexities. Everything must make common sense to me."

"Speculators have been around since the early ages. As long as any kind of market was available for free exchange of goods, services and some form of currency, speculators have been in existence. None of the early successful speculators ever had to rely on some magic formula spit out by a computer or ever had to learn new math. At its basic level, successful speculation remains unchanged from the days long gone. It still is careful observation of the market's trend, clear interpretation of the observed events and action taken with careful money management techniques relying on best odds of wins."

I asked him why he called this a disclaimer. His response was that humans are funny animals. They do not have in them to wait for years and years of learning by practice. Humans like to have an immediate answer to making big money in the markets. Most folks will refuse to spend the time, efforts, energy and money needed to learn and experience a successful method of speculation. In that respect, human beings are a lot like teenagers. They are in such a hurry to grow up that they make all kinds of stupid mistakes. Like they say, youth is wasted on the young. Similarly, in the markets, caution and prudence is wasted on the novice.

Boyd continued, "Humans will never listen to the words of caution from experienced and successful speculators. But they will blindly follow and believe a blatant bullish projection offered by a hype-filled talking head. If someone comes around and says that his prediction is that the Dow Jones Industrial will hit 20,000 by 2007, it will not be surprising to see a ton of readers flock to him. Then every time the market rallies a bit, he has to claim that this is the beginning of the trend that will take the Dow Jones Industrial all the way to 20,000. Whether or not the Industrials get there is immaterial. All he has to do is keep claiming at every rally that it is the beginning of the true move. And the gullible public will keep swallowing the pill because they do not want to miss out on the perceived big move that is coming. But if you offered the obvious and the truth that for the Dow to get to 20,000 from its current levels, the Industrials have to double in 2 years, most folks will turn a blind eye."

"Most services on the street will offer the public what they want to hear. After all, how many of us will pay a service to hear something we do not think is going to happen? How many will pay to hear caution and, perhaps, even bad news? If the reader comes to the market looking for riches, he has already formed in his mind a conclusion that the market offers riches. He has already telegraphed that he has idle funds he wishes to put to use or has funds he wishes to put at risk. Once a human has arrived at the decision that the market is the place to make good returns, he has confirmed his obvious bias that he believes that prices are headed higher. To try and convince him that is not the case is foolhardy. As that would only mean that the once convinced mind of the human has to first accept that he was wrong. And, second, he has to accept that there is no possibility of the perceived riches he had seen."

"Most importantly, all the plans the human being had of spending the riches that was going to be his from the market have now been dashed. That is way too much for any human being to handle. Psychologically, this is almost impossible for a human being to comprehend. As a result, he will actively seek out those services that will agree with him and appeal to his dreams of riches from the market."

And he went on, "Imagine that you have $100,000 sitting in the bank. Assume it is earning 2-4% depending upon the interest rate environment. But this is a safe 2-4% that is trickling in. Then you see that the stock index most commonly followed moved up 5% in one month. And you see a couple of stocks move 10-30% in a month. And you suddenly hear all the pundits talk about a great bull market that is upon us. The big noise is suddenly how the economy is on full steam. You see and hear all the hype and the buzz in the media. The internet is full of on-the-spot experts. Everybody is giving their take on the market. All one hears is that the market is going through the roof. Add in a couple of great earnings reports from a couple of companies. Suddenly you feel inadequate and feel like a fool for accepting 2-4% annual return. You think to yourself that it is foolish to be missing out on such great returns. And then on, my friend, disaster is yours to keep."

"I have been around a few cycles as you know. I started out right after the 1929 crash. And, boy, my timing was awful. I entered right near the top in 1929 and rode the elevator down all the way for three years. And when the reactionary bull market started in 1932, I had no money. It was 1936 before I had earned and saved some money and I was now ready for the market once again. And guess what happened? The 1936 - 1940 bear market hit me. By the time the early 1940s had come around, I was devastated. But the lessons I learned then have made me a very comfortable life since then as I have never lost more than an insignificant amount of what I have made in the markets. I have been able to extract large amounts from the market without giving back more than just a few pennies on the dollar. But it took the heavy losses during the ten years in the 1930s for me to learn the lessons. I can guarantee you that nobody learns the lessons unless they lose their shirts. And once you lost your shirt, there can be only one of two avenues. Most will walk away never to return. A very small percentage will take the harsh lessons learned and turn the lessons to their advantage during subsequent cycles."

"The best lesson I have learned is to rely on myself and not on anybody else. What I observe, what I interpret and what actions I take based solely on my interpretation has proven to me that I know a little something about the markets. And the one entity who has never steered me wrong is the market itself. My interpretation of the market has been more right than wrong. And that has been the key to success."

I asked Boyd about how he came about his "first, do no harm" rule. He said that the years and years it took for him to recover his losses taught him that what is lost in a year could take decades to recover. If one could avoid such devastating losses, then the battle is won from the very beginning. To illustrate, he worked out some figures and said, "Let us take our sample example account that had $100,000 to speculate in the market. If the account lost a third of its value and got down to $66,666, the account has to make back $33,333 to breakeven. That means the account has to make $33,333 on $66,666 or a 50% return just to breakeven."

"Do you know how hard it is for an account that made mistakes and ended down 33% to turn around and eliminate all the mistakes and on top of that pull off some great moves to make a 50% return on investment? In fact, what usually happens is that an account that lost a third in one year, learns some lessons and loses the following year again. But the losses in the second year will likely be smaller than the 33% loss experienced the prior year. It is a learning process. The account loses a lesser and lesser amount year after year until it starts to make money. And it starts off making small returns first before it can make big returns. Like I said, it is a long learning process. And it takes years to recover and come back to even. On the other hand, if an account only lost 5% and went from $100,000 to $95,000, it only has to make $5,000 on $95,000 investment to recover. This is a little over 5% gain that is needed to breakeven. By not losing, one can save years and years of agony, hard work, pain and sleepless nights. Not losing is worth many years of learning in the markets."

"Most entrants into the market will start off by losing. I do not mean their first trade execution will be a losing one. I am referring to one complete cycle. One complete cycle means a full up trend and a full downtrend cycle. Most folks will come out in the minus column after their first full cycle, assuming one was able to stay afloat or liquid for the entire duration of time of a complete cycle. Many will lose well before completing a full cycle. The occasional novice who starts off winning big ends up giving it all back by the time the cycle is complete."

"After a cycle or two, those who persevere and have the courage to try and study the market and, more importantly, understand the workings of the market, will learn to make initial small gains. With time and more experience, study and discipline, finally the participant graduates to being a speculator. Add more time, experience, discipline and patience - suddenly the speculator reaches the upper echelons of a master speculator. After all the years of learning, a master speculator comes to understand the simplicity and the complexities of the market. He learns to keep his plan of execution simple and he accepts that the market is very complex."

I asked Boyd a simple set of questions at this point. I said, "You know, my experiences with the public has been mixed. They either love my candor or hate it. There is no middle ground. I have found that when I simplify the market's actions and talk in terms of probability of wins, they either get it or they do not. Again, there is no middle ground. How do you express your take on the market without making waves with your readers?"

Boyd was smiling. As I said, he was in a more cheerful mood that morning. He sipped his coffee, thought for a moment and replied, "I know exactly what you are saying. I have seen cycles and cycles of booms and busts since the 1930s. And dealing with the markets is just as good as dealing with people because the market is nothing but people buying and selling stocks to and from each other. It is the sum total of all types of folks interacting with each other. Observing the market is nothing but observing people. The drawback for me is that I am not a great people person."

"However, I have been blessed with the gift of observing and interpreting the market correctly. Well, I take that back. I am more right than I am wrong. And I always approach the market with the complete awareness that I may be wrong in my interpretation of the market's direction. The fact that I am not correct all the time tells me that the smart money or the smartest folks do not agree with me all the time. Which is about the same thing you said when you suggested that folks either loved your writing or hated it. That is what makes the market. You are either right or wrong. When you are right, the folks who are wrong will not see things your way. When you are wrong, folks who are right will not see things your way. As a result, it should not surprise you at all about the blow-hot blow-cold reception your writings get."

"Buyers and sellers come together to establish the price of a stock. Buyers are buying as they believe in higher prices to come. Sellers are selling because they are anticipating lower prices. Obviously only one group is going to be right. It is not possible for both buyers and sellers to be right at the same time for any extended periods of time. If the buyers are right, prices will move higher. If the sellers are right, prices will move lower. The market is very simple. We humans make it more complicated by trying to figure out a system to beat the market. Instead, if we just focus on being in sync with the market, life will be much easier."

"We try to look for a magic answer to finding the gold at the end of the rainbow. And we try to find a rainbow everyday of the week, every week of the year, year after year. We forget that rainbows do not come everyday of the week. The Wall Street machinery of tipsters, bullish newsletters, stock brokers, rumor mongers, insiders, agents of the insiders, etc. all work individually and in concert with each other to convince us that rainbows come about every day. One has to wait for rainbows to develop. It requires patience and the ability to sit tight and do nothing."

"It is about the hardest lesson to learn to wait and sit tight and to do nothing. To await the right conditions and confirmation of improved probabilities of wins is not possible for the vast majority of the public. Wall Street would cease to exist if all the folks decided not to buy and just sit tight and await better days. That would be the end of Wall Street. That cannot be acceptable to the cutting edge machinery of pure unadulterated form of capitalism. The machinery will keep churning out plenty of useless information, misinformation, disinformation, hype, rumor, etc., to keep bringing in a continuous flow of buyers irrespective of the prevailing conditions. There is a sale made available every day. Not a single broker has been found to be in existence who will say to anyone at any time the famous non-existing words in the broker lingo, 'Do not buy today. Wait for a better day.' These words do not exist in Wall Street's vocabulary."

I was not surprised that Boyd could explain things in a unique manner. He had that gift. So I decided to pursue the matter further and asked him, "I know I do not have to be concerned with educating your readers. They are savvy folks like you who have been around for a while and know the game well. What, if anything, would you suggest I keep foremost in my mind so that I do not lose focus. I am not as well-versed with the market's tricks as you are. At the basic level and under the rule of 'first, do no harm,' what specific thoughts can you add that will work for me? You know me well and perhaps there is something you can add to help me be more disciplined."

He thought for a second and said, "I think you are quite disciplined as you are. The only thing I can add is that you must keep in mind that the stock market is nothing but a game of treasure hunt. If you can keep that in mind, you will be focused and will not get side-tracked. I first used the example of a treasure hunt to explain the market to my daughter when she was just a young girl. I found that she has to this day remembered the explanation and she was able to grasp the workings of the market at an age when most do not even know what a trend is."

"The market is a game of treasure hunt. All players are given a set of clues. As it happens, the clues offered to all of the players are the same. If correctly deciphered, the first set of clues will take the participant to a second set of clues at the first mile-post. Then, if the clues at the first mile-post are correctly deciphered, the participant can get to the second mile-post where additional clues will be available. Thus, a participant who can consistently figure out the clues correctly will go from one mile-post to the next until he reaches the treasure. How quickly and correctly one can decipher the clues will determine who will get the treasure. Among the clues offered, some will be red herrings and false clues meant to mislead the players. And once again, the players who can recognize these misleading clues to be red herrings will be the ones with the best chance to land the treasure."

"Among the players, there will be a very small set of really extremely smart players who will have no trouble reading the clues correctly. They will decipher each and every clue along their path to the treasure correctly and at the same time they will be able to discard the misleading clues. These smart folks will be the ones to get to the treasure first and are called 'smart money'. And then there will be another very small set of players who will decipher most of the clues correctly and when they are unable to decipher the tricky clues or the misleading clues, they will just follow the 'smart money' who get everything right. Since this second group will follow the smart money, the smart money will try and mislead their followers by showing some fake-outs and shake-outs to shake-off the followers. The treasure trove is large and there is enough for most who get there sooner rather than later. Many will never get there. Some will get there late. The smart money gets there first. And many folks from the set of followers of the smart money will also get there, albeit slightly behind the smart money."

"It is no different in the market. The smart money recognizes the trend first and acts on it. Then the small set of followers will follow the smart money successfully and recognize the trend next. Most others will miss the best part of the trend. Many will come late to the party and will only be there for the brawls that come about at the end of a long party."

"The biggest problem one faces in the market is the need to wait to confirm the trend. The most common and costly mistake is to jump at every first inkling of a rally. In the stampede to be the first to identify a trend, many get crushed. It is the patient ones who wait out the many false starts, who will be fit as a fiddle to make the move when the true trend starts. A lot of money has been lost in trying to be the first one to identify the trend."

"What drew me to you is the fact that you have the courage to sit tight and not jump for every trap and temptation the market throws at us. It is a lost art and very few of us old-timers are around to remind the young ones of the dangers of the market. Everyone claims that this a new market and thus new strategies and new models are a better fit. I have forgotten how many times I have heard that since my teenage years. Every market cycle brings with it these new market strategies that are purported to be able to beat the new changed market. But the market never changes because human emotions never change when it comes to money. There is absolutely nothing new in the market. Every trick and system has been tried before in one form or another."

"I am even more convinced that you are a good fit for my readers as you will call it as you see it without mincing words. It does not matter if they agree with you or not. What they want is an honest and candid interpretation of what you observe in the market. What they are looking for is a view of the market from a speculator. They can confirm whether your interpretation is right or wrong on their own by their own test-buys or test-sells in the market. If their first positions make money, then the market will prove that the interpretation called was correct."

We went on to discuss about some of the basics of the market and Boyd ended the discussion for that morning at that point. I took my notes and headed home. It was the beginning of a long but extremely rewarding few days for me.

## Summary:

First, do not lose. Do not try to be the first to see the trend. Most first signs are wrong signs. Wait for confirming signals before making any commitments. Making headway in the market is like a game of treasure hunt.

# CHAPTER 4
## WHEN IN DOUBT, DO NOTHING

I had started writing down daily in my journal all the rules and lessons as offered by a master speculator. I would return home from my breakfast meetings with Boyd and immediately pull out the notes I had made and start typing on my lap-top. I knew if I did not put it on my computer, I would not be fully able to understand the scrappy notes I had hurriedly jotted down while Boyd was speaking. If I did not expand and place the thoughts on my computer promptly, I was afraid my short memory would lose the vital information I was being given.

I knew full well a good percentage of what I wrote down probably would still not make sense to a good many folks. After all, the market machinery had brain-washed the public into looking for cheap stocks, easy money, quick gains, short-cuts and the feel of superiority. And the genius of the marketing machinery was to imply that the novice or even a self-proclaimed professional was very smart. And since he was very smart, he would then take lessons and courses in all the techno-mumbo-jumbo and mathematical models. Then one is sold on the idea that the ability to use long words and intelligent sounding jargon would somehow help the gullible to beat the market. We humans all love to believe we are smarter than the crowd.

The genius in the marketing machine is to feed our need to feel smart. And once we are convinced that we are smarter than the average Joe because we are now so well-versed in the techno-mumbo-jumbo, we are supposedly on our way to riches. Of course, along the long journey to nowhere, we are sold on more cutting edge tools that will help us beat the market even more. And as pigs head to slaughter, we blindly fall for the sophisticated

31

salesmanship. The average Joe who comes into the market without any experience or workings of the huge Wall Street machinery has no chance.

I knew I was not that smartest cookie around. But I had learned through my own years of experiences in the markets, both in stocks and in commodities, that I was smart enough to grasp the game. I had recognized the larger picture and the over-all workings of the market. I knew now that the market was always right. And I had learned that since the market is always right, I really did not need anything else to be successful in the market, besides my ability to observe the market's action and then interpret the action. I had subconsciously become a speculator. I had not even known when the transformation had occurred. It had occurred slowly over many years after many losses. It was only when Boyd had defined what a speculator is, that I had recognized myself to be one. As they say, "it takes one to recognize one."

I had now reached a point where I was extremely picky when I would enter the market. I could wait for months on end without a trade execution. I could now easily brush aside the calls I got from brokers and tipsters and rumor mongers who would hype me on the next big thing since Cisco, Home Depot or Taser. I would just pass up all these great opportunities so that other unfortunate souls could make the big bucks. I was more interested in not losing. I did not mind losing out on a stock I would never have bought in the first place. How can I lose something that I do not have? On the other hand, I would hate losing on a stock I had to buy. Since I only bought when I could not find a reason not to buy, I would be very careful in placing my trades.

This brings me to the second lesson that Boyd covered that week. He called it simply, "when in doubt, do nothing." It sounded simple enough. But it had taken me years of large losses to get there. And I learned from Boyd's trade journals, where he recorded each and every trade he had executed, he had grasped this crucial lesson only after losses spanning over a decade in the 1930s.

There is more useless and unimportant information in the market than there is useful information. The market is full of red herrings. As we know, red herrings are used to confuse hunting dogs by throwing them off the main trail. There is no other endeavor on this planet where there is more useless, false and misleading information than in the hunt for stock market riches. But, of course, most folks do not know that because as discussed, we all like to feel like we know better. We are all really smart, much smarter than the market. That sense of knowing more than the average Joe is flamed by the machinery at every instant and we start to firmly believe it.

I asked Boyd, "I hear people claim that timing the market cannot be done and that one should be fully invested through years and years to reap the benefits of the stock market. What do you make of that?"

He replied, "I have a hard time accepting such nonsense. If I had held on to stocks through cycles and cycles of bull and bear markets, I would have been incredibly lucky to come out just about even after decades of fully being invested. The machinery wants the common folks to keep buying and buying through bull and bear trends because the machinery exists to sell stocks. If no buyers can be found, the machinery has to cease to exist and that is not acceptable. Therefore, the brain-washing goes on that the market cannot be timed."

"While it is impossible to pick the absolute bottom and the absolute top of a significant trend, I can definitely catch the meat of a significant move. During such significant trends, odds of winning improve substantially and my test case buys prove to me when such improved odds come about. Once proven that odds have improved, I can then seriously and deliberately expose larger commitments to the market. And I keep moving my sell-stops along an up trending and moving stock up along with its price. This way, at some point when odds of continued trend start to diminish, my sell-stops start getting hit and I get taken out of the market. And usually odds start to diminish in advance of the end of the trending move. And I may not be able to catch the top, but as I said, I am happy with the middle meaty portion of a significant move. Just because the vast majority cannot accomplish this does not mean it cannot be done. It takes discipline and a systematic approach."

"Another key point is to remember what we old-timers say - do not let the wish become the father of the thought. Just because one wishes the market to go up should not turn into the thought that the market is indeed going up. Do not see what is not there. Look for confirming signals. And when confirming signals are absent or there is doubt about the trend, then do nothing. The market is a genius at offering false signals. Until I can see that the trend has been confirmed by the indices as well as leading young growth stocks, I have a hard time placing my test-case small commitments. I can only get my signals from the indices in conjunction with leading stocks. If I cannot get a confirmation, I must assume the market is throwing a curve ball."

## Summary:

The wish cannot be the father of the thought. Do not try to see something that is not there. The fact that you have free funds available to place in the market does not mean that the market is ready to offer you opportunities for gains.

# CHAPTER 5
## HOW TO SPECULATE

Speculation has three components to it. Observation, Interpretation, Action. The way Boyd covered each and every segment was so simple that it was hard to comprehend why most folks cannot be successful in speculation. Then that thought passed quickly as I recognized the human failings we all have are what cause over 90% of our losses in the marketplace.

Observation involves watching some of the basics that go on in the market. The basics boil down to looking for a sign of changed trend or changed conditions. When one is not "in" the market, one is sitting and waiting to get "in." How to determine that the tide has changed and it is time to get in? First, we must always start from the point where we are out of the market. Nobody comes to the market being already in. Besides a small insignificant fortunate ones who get handed a large inheritance, most of us come to the market on our own volition. But as we approach the market we have taken the first step of setting up a trading account with some brokerage firm.

Before embarking on our first decision to buy or not to buy, we must face some of the basic questions. Among them are - what type of an account do we have? Is it a margin account? If so, at what point does the margin account use margin to buy? Will the account start using margin from the get go? Or can we insist which executions can use margin funds? This is very important because we cannot get into margin funds from the get go. Without a firm handle on learning the ropes, borrowing (margin funds is borrowed funds from the broker) can be the first culprit in killing an account right away. From a practical point of view, margin should not come until and unless one can accept and live with the losses on margin which amplify losses quickly. For more about margin rules, one should first spend a few minutes talking to their brokerage before even thinking of opening an account.

It is best to open an account where the account holder has full authority to identify which trades can use margin funds. Some brokerages do not allow the account holder to dictate which trades can be on margin. And they end up placing each trade on margin funds (if the stock is margin-able). That is a dangerous way to work with a broker. All decisions about everything on the account should always be with the account holder.

Having set-up a trading account, it then is the brokerage's job to market to us every service they have. We will be offered special rates if we trade more frequently. We will be offered "in depth research" and the "market guru's take on the market." We will be offered "guidance." All of a sudden the amount of "help" available to us is unimaginable. We are everybody's best friend and we get all kinds of "free stuff."

Boyd always said that he had to develop a detachment and distance from listening to the brokers and the market insiders. In order to do that, he would refuse all input from the insiders. Anybody who has even an appearance of conflict with the thought, "can he ever tell me to just stay in cash," was an insider. If somebody could not tell us to stay put and not to spend our money, then he likely was an insider. It was a simple screen. If somebody could not tell us to our face, "there is nothing good to buy right now and wait for better conditions," then the red-flag should go up that such a person is an insider and chances are that there is a big conflict of interest. Boyd had developed a simple system to stay away from the noise. He never watched TV, never read stock reports, never listened to ratings or analysts, he never paid attention to what others said and he paid attention only to leading stocks and market indices. His take was, as mentioned before, "the market is the only one who is always right." Everybody else is wrong most of the time and right only occasionally.

Having an account set up with a broker does not mean an action has to be immediately taken. In fact, one should start to observe the market for some period. Observation is best on charts. Some folks have no use for charts and others swear by charts. Like all things in life, the real use is somewhere in between the two extremes. The only importance of a chart is that it shows what the market and stocks have been doing in the recent past. It helps us figure out if the indices or stocks are moving up or moving down or moving but getting nowhere. Observation is the first step in speculation. To observe what the current conditions are, one must take a look at charts to see where the indices and stocks were weeks ago, months ago, years ago, etc. If something is visible on daily charts and weekly charts, then odds are higher that whatever is being observed is actually happening. If something is visible on daily charts but unclear on weekly charts, then we need more data to see what is going on. If something is not clear, then we assume that nothing is happening that is worth exposing our funds to the markets.

In order to begin to understand a change of trend, Boyd started with the simple basics. A trend is in place unless it is definitely reversed. If an up trend is in effect, for example, it continues to be in place unless reversed with confirming signs. Similarly, a down-trend is in effect and continues to be in place unless reversed with confirming signs. If a trend-less market is in effect, it is assumed to remain in effect until a firm trend is established with confirming signs.

It takes time for the market to establish a trend. And it takes time for the trend to be reversed. Everything in the market takes time. Learning takes time. Making gains takes time. Even losing big takes time because the market will occasionally offer small crumbs as gains to remove the fear and instill hope, greed and over-confidence. The big knockout only comes about after landing some small, significant but withstand-able blows.

To observe a change of trend, a few basic events must occur. For simplicity, we will assume that we are trying to observe a changed trend from a current existing down-trend to a new reversed up trend. We know that a downtrend is a series of lower highs and lower lows. So the first sign would be a rally off the most recent low. It is a fine line between believing every rally off a recent low is a new bull trend to allowing for the chance that every rally off the most recent low may be the first sign of a changed trend.

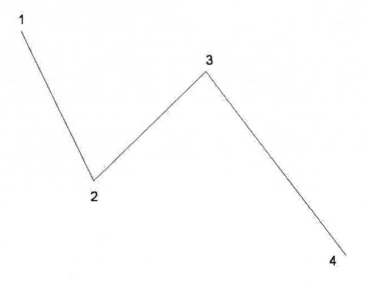

**Figure 5a. A down trending market**

1 = prior down trend

2 = most recent low

3 = reactionary high to the most recent low

4 = a new lower low

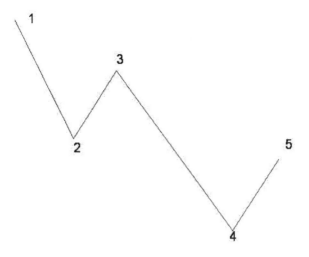

**Figure 5b. A potential changed trend may or may not be in the offing**

1 = prior down trend

2 = most recent low

3 = reactionary high to the most recent low

4 = a new lower low

5 = a rally off of point 4

Obviously, figure 5a is a down trending market. Let us assume that figure 5a is potentially near the end of a down-trending market. We have discussed previously that not every rally off the most recent low is a bull trend. And we have also discussed that while not accepting every rally to be the beginning of a rally, one must start observing the market and other confirming signs for a true changed trend. So let us then proceed to figure 5b. The rally off the low at point 4 could be, but yet to be proved to be, the beginning of a new changed trend. A few days after the point 4 is pegged, let us assume the index is now at point 5 within the figure 5b. Besides knowing that a few days' rally has ensued there is not much else we know at this point.

But since we are observing, we are paying attention at this point to stocks that are making new highs, especially new all time highs. Since the true leaders in any confirmed rally are the new young growth stocks that make new all time highs, we have to focus in on the new young unknown growth stocks for a clear picture.

In my report on Taser's run, "The Perfect Stock," I had gone into considerable detail of the way the insiders on the Street work. But as I had said before, regrettably the message had been lost on many readers. The big moves in the market occur in the new young cutting edge companies with great potential earnings growth and great anticipated earnings growth. The move is more or less fully underway well before earnings actually show up on a company's balance sheet. And many times a stock tops out near its peak earnings growth. That is because the market is forward looking and everything is discounted months, if not years, in advance.

In addition, I had gone on to show the workings of the investment bankers or the underwriters and other insider groups in the way a stock is moved up during a confirmed market up-trend. Here again, the message was lost. Probably yet again due to my shortcomings as a writer. But the main point I had made was that insiders are large holders of stock when the stock becomes public. They cannot sell large amounts of stock early on in a stock's life or close to an IPO date. The stock has to be first worked and moved up and up and higher and higher in price to accommodate the large selling that needs to be done by the insiders. If the insiders start selling large number of shares, the stock gets depressed easily and the price that the large insiders get for their sale is low and the stock has no chance of being fully distributed into a wide array of holders. The stock has to be worked and moved up and down by the insiders to help distribute the stock into a large diverse group of holders so that no one set of holders can get control of the company. This is a long and laborious process and usually takes years to accomplish. The bigger point I was trying to cover was that such successful stock operations occur rarely. Of the hundreds of IPOs that come to the market, only a handful ever go on to make a solid move.

As a general rule, though, the big move of a trending stock comes during a relatively short period of time. Once the true move has started, the insiders will ensure it is fully played out before the market's primary trend changes. In majority of the cases, the true move of a stock starts, endures and comes to an end within one up cycle in the general market.

So, the only way to confirm that a potential rally is beginning a true changed trend is to start observing new young growth companies making all time new highs. Since we know for a fact that the insiders can only work a stock to its best portion of an up trend during a confirmed market up cycle, we can safely say odds are very low that a new up cycle will endure in the general market without the accompanying set of new young growth stocks making a big run.

At this point of discussions, Boyd informed me that he would like to cover the general market's basics about a potential change of trend first and then in the ensuing days he would cover the confirming signs as offered by individual stocks. He added that individual stocks will confirm the beginning of a true primary trend in the general market, just as they will confirm the end of the true up trend in the general market. He said that leading individual stocks will confirm the market's primary trend. I was told that the simplicity would become clear in the coming days.

Before we went on to figure 5c, Boyd advised me that the figure 5b was crucial. He said that what one observes during the segment between point 4 and point 5 was critical. If there was confirmation from individual stocks during this segment, then odds were increasing that we may have seen the low of the market for the foreseeable future. But he said that I would have to wait for another day to get into individual stocks as there was still some work needed to be done on the general market indices.

In figure 5c, Boyd completed figure 5b with a little bit more information. From point 4 the index rallied to point 6. Then, after pegging a near-term high at point 6, the market reacted down to point 7. But point 7 was a higher low than the prior low at point 4. Thus the first higher low was pegged. This was a significant sign that indeed the market may have changed its trend from a down-trend to an up trend. Boyd went on to add an additional segment to figure 5b in figure 5c and added the segment from point 7 to point 8. He said that as soon as point 8 went slightly above point 6 as shown in figure 5c, there was now a clear sign that indeed there had been a change of trend. He said that from point 4 forward, we had seen a complete set of higher highs and higher lows. Point 7 was a higher low than point 4. And when point 8 was penetrated to the upside above point 6, we had thus seen a higher high as well. A full set of a higher high and a higher low, therefore, indicated a changed trend.

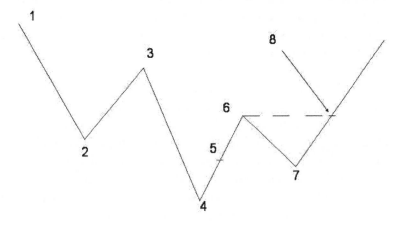

**Figure 5c. A change of trend**

1 = prior down trend

2 = most recent low

3 = reactionary high to the most recent low

4 = a new lower low

5 = a rally off the most recent low

6 = a high pegged during the most recent rally

7 = a downward reaction to the most recent rally, but this low is higher than the prior low at point 4

8 = as price reaches above point 6, the prior high, a new changed trend is indicated

And at this point, Boyd drew figure 5d and said that this final figure confirmed a full fledged up-trend was in progress. It was then he added that this was a very simplified version of a potential change of trend. But it was completely feasible and possible to see improved conditions during the segment between point 4 and point 5 if only one knew what to look for. This is where individual stocks would come into play.

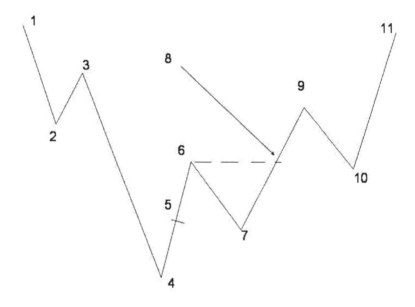

**Figure 5d. A change of trend is confirmed**

1 = prior down trend

2 = most recent low

3 = reactionary high to the most recent low

4 = a new lower low

5 = a rally off the most recent low

6 = a high pegged during the most recent rally

7 = a downward reaction to the most recent rally, but this low is higher than the prior low at point 4

8 = as price reaches above point 6, the prior high, a new changed trend is indicated

9 = a new higher high above the prior high at point 6 is pegged

10 = a higher low than the prior low at point 7 is pegged

11 = a new higher high continues the up trend

## Summary:

Not every rally is the beginning of an up trend. But at every rally, one must be open to the possibility that a new up trend had begun. One must start looking for confirming signs from new young growth stocks making all time new highs.

# CHAPTER 6
## CONFIRM EVERYTHING

I had learned over and over again that the market has a great ability to fool us humans. Boyd used to say that the market fools everybody most of the time. The business of trying to predict the market moves was flawed. About as flawed as trying to predict one's own future. About a third of the market forecasters are right about a third of the time. And even if they are, by chance, right about the direction, they then go on to be wrong about the timing. Forecasting is a poor way to operate within the market. And that is what most folks do. They try and predict and pay the price dearly.

A successful speculator interprets and does not predict. We covered the basics of interpretation of a changed trend based solely on the general market index action. But, we have to confirm everything in the market because there are way too many red herrings. If one went back to our original figure 5b and takes a look at point 5, we will recall that we are at a point where the market has the possibility of a changed trend. At point 5 in figure 5b, the market has rallied off the most recent low for a few days. On daily charts as well weekly charts the last low pegged has not been under-cut. This is the point in time that we start looking for confirming signs from individual stocks.

But before we start looking at each individual stocks, we must cover some of the basics. We are, like all market participants, only interested in stocks that are going to move up in price. I had gone to great lengths in making the case for buying into stocks that make all time new highs in my report on Taser's run, "The Perfect Stock." I realize now that perhaps my explanations were too lengthy. So I asked Boyd to explain how stocks making new

45

highs keeping making new higher highs during a confirmed market up-trend. As it turned out his was a simpler explanation.

He said that any new confirmed market up-trend must have a new set of unknown young growth stocks that lead the market. Every cycle has new leaders. It is not unlike a sports team. It takes a new generation of young players to take a game to new heights after a set of older prior greats start to slow down. In the early industrial revolution days, it was steel and rails that led the market up. Then came the autos and heavy machines. Then came the airplane and associated industries. Then came radio and television and associated technologies. Then came computers. Then came software and then the internet and associated technologies. In there somewhere were medical technologies and pharmaceuticals. The next serious bull trend will have a new set of leaders. It always takes a new set of leaders to carry the market forward.

I interrupted him and said, "But you say that one should be realistic and should not be expecting more than 3 or 4 tradable segments of confirmed up trend in any 10-year cycle in the markets. Would that not mean that there will be vast periods of inactivity? In such periods what is happening to the new young growth stocks you are watching and waiting for to make their move?"

Boyd took a sip on his coffee and took a second to put his thought together and explained casually, "I am one of those people who approaches the market with a degree of skepticism. I start with the assumption that every rally is a fake out . Until this assumption of mine has been disproved by individual stocks, I am not convinced of the rally's strength. To answer your question, yes, the big money is possible only in about 3-4 up-trend segments in any 10-year cycle. During the waiting time, these new young growth stocks are setting up their play. The set-up takes a long time. To wait for such cycles to make serious and large commitments is hard for most folks. But if one took the time to review their own past executions and performance over the recent most 10-year cycle, they will note that more than 80% of the folks have lost money in the market. Anyone can have a good and a lucky year. That is not the test. The true test of a successful speculator is how he did over a 10-year period. If one has the guts to dig out their own 10-year performance and do a study, they will easily recognize that what was made was more than offset by what was lost."

"During the down time I have my charts always with me and I am always on the look out for the next big runner. At any given moment I could be watching tens of different stocks but with a serious focus on only about 5-10 stocks. I know what I am looking for and I know a winner when I see one. It is only how capable I am in placing my commitments and trading the winner most effectively along its quickest and farthest part of the move that determines my degree of success. I have had years where I had the right stocks but I was not able to effectively trade them due to severe shake-outs and fake-outs. In other years, I have been able to trade the big winners very effectively. On the whole, I aim to catch a handful of serious big moves during any 10-year cycle. I say to my daughter that if I double my money four or five times in a decade and then if I do not give much of it back to the market, then I have done my job. For example, if I started with $100,000 and doubled my money only 3 times during a 10-year cycle during three different up trending cycles and then never lost anything during the rest of the 10-year cycle, my $100,000 would be worth $800,000. Not bad for a 10-year performance. Let us assume one did this over two ten-year cycles. The $100,000 would be worth $6,400,000."

"My philosophy is simple. The first premise is that the stock market is very tricky and more than 80% of the participants will lose money over the long-term. If I am going to be involved with an animal that defeats 80% of the folks, then I am only interested in the big money. In other words, if I am going to risk losing in the market, I better be looking only for the big bucks. Otherwise, why risk my money for meager wins or worse, to take losses?"

"The second premise is that the big bucks is made only on young unknown growth stocks. The old vanguards like General Motors, IBM, Wal-Mart, Cisco, Microsoft, etc., have become mature stocks with large floats and are more for the pension funds and others who believe they can withstand the gyrations of the market via steady companies. Little do they know that one single bear run will wipe away all the hard earned gains made over many years. But everybody is different and everybody comes to the market with different attitudes and goals."

"The third premise is that the stock I am watching as the potential winner must have shown to me via its price/volume action that it has the ability to move up in price. If I am a ball club owner, why would I pay a ball-player the big bucks unless I see during the minor leagues stint that he was consistently good and was in fact improving his averages. If I cannot see such improving or rising ability, I have no interest in a stock. Which is what I refer to as the prior up trend. Without a prior up trend, a stock has not proven anything to me."

"With thousands of stocks moving up and moving down, how to narrow my focus down to the next big winners? Well, I start off with only those stocks that are 10-15 years old or younger. In other words, I have no interest in stocks that have been in existence for over 15 years. As I said, it is the new young growth companies that make the big bucks. If a stock is over 15 years old, it has had the chance to move in prior bull trends. And if a stock has made a move in prior bull trends, then it is probably too late for me to catch its fastest and farthest move up."

"Then I demand that the stock I am watching is nearing its all time high. Some folks look for stocks making new 52-week highs. But not me. I need to see a stock come near its all time high. My interest is first and foremost to watch as few stocks as possible. Which means I must cut down the number of potential winners down to a humanly manageable level. For me to do this, I have to place certain restrictions and parameters in place. So, all the parameters I use are for the sole goal of reducing the number of stocks that I watch to just a handful. After all, we started with the aim of looking for just a handful of clear big winners during any given decade."

"I think I mentioned somewhere that everything in the stock market takes time. It takes time to make or lose big money. It takes time for a stock to set up its play before making its move. During the course of its set-up, many times a stock will offer many false signals. It may offer signs that a true move has begun, only to reverse and head back into its basing or the setting-up phase. It will demand patience from the speculator. Since the speculator is waiting for the one clear stretch of 6-12 month-period where the stock is going to zoom at its fastest pace and go the farthest, he is only interested in a clear-cut visible trend where the stock makes a clean set of higher highs and higher lows. Such a move usually only comes about once during any stock's lifetime. During such a period, it is not unusual to see a stock multiply many times over its beginning price for the time period."

"You wrote a nice little book about Taser's run of 7000% in 12 months, which explained some of the greatest lessons of the stock market. But I think you will be disappointed to know that the lessons in your book will only be recognized by the true speculators. The general public will completely miss the lessons. That only proves the point that truly successful speculators are a silent and almost non-existent minority in the market. Since the number of true speculators is minimal in the marketplace, I am afraid your book will not sell as many copies as the run-of-the-mill book that touts the stock market as the greatest thing since the invention of the wheel."

"To simplify the lesson, I like to see stocks that use up many many months or even years in setting up their play. The longer the sideways basing pattern and the longer the quiet unnoticed set-up, the faster and farthest the move when the true move begins. I can tell you that the general public has no patience in waiting for the play to be set-up. That is where the big mistake is made by the public. They will believe every breakout from one price range into another is the beginning of a great new move. To explain this I have to take a step back and go into what breakouts are."

"You will find a dime a dozen services out there claiming to know what breakout stocks are and how they behave. Unfortunately, not one of them will do justice to its readers. The implication by the Wall Street machinery is that when stocks breakout, many will make a good run-up. This implication is either naive or purposely misleading. Whatever the case may be, it is a false premise. First of all, one must define clearly what is meant by a breakout. A breakout just means that a stock or an index broke out of one trading range and went into another trading range. That is it. Nothing more is meant by a breakout. There is a wide following and belief that a breakout is the beginning of an up-trend. To assume, claim or imply such a thing is foolishness. A breakout occurs during some point of an every up trend. That does not mean every breakout is the beginning of an up trend. A great major league ball player starts off in the minor leagues. It does not follow that every minor league player goes on to become a great ball player."

"An up trend is a series of higher highs and higher lows. A stock that is in an up-trend, shows along its up-trend some consolidation periods where the stock rests. Once that rest has been taken, the stock resumes its up trend. In such a case one can say that the breakout from the resting phase began a new up trend. It is only such rare few breakouts that confirm and carry on an up-trend, which are the true breakouts in my book."

"In any given year, it is not unusual to see 500 or more breakouts by stocks making new highs. In a good year, that number may even double to over a thousand stocks breaking out to new highs. And at the exact point of such a breakout, every stock looks good for that one moment when the stock is breaking out. But these are 52-week highs. I am only interested in stocks making all time highs. And I am only interested in stocks that are already in an up trend. That means, I am only interested in new young growth companies that are already showing rising prices and in new all time high price areas."

"To sum it up, I am looking for stocks that have spent some years and months in a long sideways basing pattern. This is the set up. Longer the set up, better the odds of a good move coming up when the play actually begins. Then the stock must enter into all time new price highs and show a tendency of rising prices for some weeks and months. Typically, I only look at stocks that have already doubled from its low to high for the latest 52 week period. In other words, if I check for the 52-week low and the 52-week high price of a stock, the 52-week high price must be at the very least twice the price of its 52-week low price. In addition, I must see at least one resting phase during the up trend or the game-phase. As I said, the game begins only after a long set up."

"I then add an additional requirement. The stock must have moved at the very least 20% or more in price from the high of its last breakout within four weeks or less. This 20% move within four weeks must have occurred without the stock ever heading back into the consolidation price area. Then I call this stock my 20/4 mover - which stands for 20% or more within 4 weeks without heading back into the basing or the consolidation price area."

At this point, Boyd took out his note pad and drew a figure as shown below in figure 6. And there on the figure, he indicated the long base or the set up phase. Then he indicated the prior up trend phase of the beginning of the game-phase. He also marked down the first rest period or the consolidation phase. On top of the consolidation area, he indicated the 20/4 type move to call this type of stock his 20/4 mover. As usual, I picked up his illustration and inserted it into my folder which held my notes. Once again, Boyd's figure was simple, easy and genius in its explanation of his terminology. I took a look at the figure as shown on figure 6 and everything Boyd explained that morning was easy to understand.

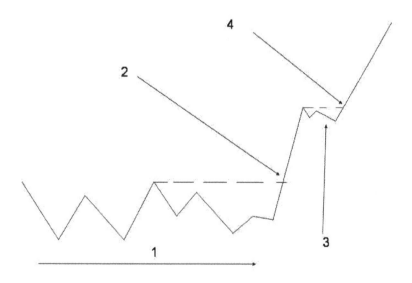

**Figure 6. A typical 20/4 type stock move**

1 = long basing phase lasting months and years

2 = all time new price highs are pegged

3 = consolidation or resting phase

4 = break out to new highs to proceed to make 20% or more move within four weeks from point 4 onward

Boyd's mind was working at an astonishing clip that morning. As I said, on that morning he was quite cheerful and if I had not known, it would have been easy to forget that the clock was winding down for him. He was as sharp as ever. I decided to take full advantage of that day as I realized that such nice days were numbered for him and that I may never get another day like this one with him. So I never interrupted him for the duration of the lesson as morning turned into afternoon. We squeezed in a light lunch and continued on with matters relating to confirming signals in the market.

Boyd continued with ease as words came out easily for him. He was in his element and I could easily picture him placing his trade executions with the cool, calm, detached and calculating demeanor he projected.

He said, "While the first stock that makes such a 20/4 type move is a good sign, I usually wait until I see at least two such stocks from two separate industries that show me that the time has come to test the waters in the market. I have not really talked about the importance of volume here. I will reserve the importance of volume for later. Now that I have seen at least two 20/4 moving stocks that meet my required criteria, I will then make the decision that it is time to test the market with small pilot buys. A small pilot buy is a test buy in the market to confirm what I have seen, observed and interpreted is correct. If I am indeed correct, then my test buys or pilot buys should make gains from the get go without getting below my buy prices. In order to confirm that I am right, I need to implement one other action. This is the stop-loss rule. This is well talked about, well written about and widely followed by traders and speculators. Some do it successfully and others do it badly. But at least traders and speculators do follow some form of a stop-loss. That is better than what the gamblers and investors do who have no stop-loss policy."

"I think you did a good enough job in explaining the principles of stop-loss in your Taser report. I do not believe there is much to add to what you have already covered well. The basic idea of a stop-loss is two-fold. The first goal is to protect our capital. This you covered in your book and others have as well in many books that are out on the market. The second more important goal is to prove me wrong. When several of my sell-stops get hit, the market is sending a message to me that I am wrong in my interpretation of the market's and the stock's direction."

"Coming back to my 20/4 type stocks, I place a sell-stop at my buy prices as soon as a stock makes a 20/4 type move. Thus if a stock that moves 20% or more within four weeks from its breakout and then turns and comes back to my buy price, I get sold out. I do this as the odds of a 20/4 type stock coming back to its buy price are minimal if the market is in an up trend. As I said, the stop is to help me prove whether I am right or wrong in my take on the market's direction. On the other hand, stocks that run up 20% or more within 4 weeks of their breaking out to new highs, usually have just begun their true big move. These stocks act as the true indicators or confirming stocks of the market's trend. In addition, psychologically, I am prepping myself all the time to accept that no 20/4 type stock will ever show me a loss. This way I have an in-built affinity for such stocks."

As Boyd continued on this topic, I decided to split my notes for that day into two halves. I realized that there was a lot of information coming my way on that day. I did not want my mind to start to wander and lose some of the minute details in Boyd's lessons. I decided to ask him for a few minutes break at this point to allow me to gather my thoughts and to allow me to organize my notes.

## Summary:

It is always the new young unknown growth companies that confirm the market's trend. Usually the set up of the true move takes a long time for individual stocks. Look for stocks that came to the market within the most recent 10-15 years. Then look for stocks that have gone sideways for long periods of many months or years in what is called at the set-up phase.  Once the stock being watched makes it into the all time high price area, one must confirm to see that its 52 week high is at least twice its 52 week low.  This allows the speculator to reject all but only the true big potential winners.  Once the stock has made it into the new all time price area, look for it to make a 20% move within four weeks after breaking out of a consolidation area.  This is what can be called one's 20/4 type stocks.  It is then that one should sit up and starting to pay attention to the market as well as to individual stocks.  It is then time to consider coming back into the market.

# CHAPTER 7
## VOLUME IS JUST ABOUT EVERYTHING

Boyd said that the signs offered by the volume of shares traded was just about everything. I was well aware of the importance of price and volume action of a stock and of the general market indices. But the way Boyd looked at me when he made that statement about volume signaled to me that there was more of a lesson there than most will ever know. So I asked him to elaborate on the basics of volume of trade.

Boyd said, "When most people hear me talk about the importance of volume of trade, they usually have no clue about what I am talking about. They usually dismiss the importance of volume of trade or have no idea how to see the volume of trade on a chart. To me volume is all important. When I see a stock's chart, I can immediately get a snap-shot of where the stock is in its potential move. It is absolutely very important for me to pay attention to volume. As simple as volume of trade may seem at first glance, the trick is to be vigilant and diligent so as to not fall for false signals."

"Seeing something that is not there is the most common and the most expensive mistake even the most experienced speculators make. It is easy to rationalize one's position by seeing something that is not there. The need to be right makes one biased in seeing what they want to see. And then the wish becomes the father of the thought. And wishing a move to occur makes one see things that are not there. I write often in my comments that the market is a mirage. One sees water where there is sand if one is thirsty enough. Then as one sees what is not there, just like the unfortunate soul lost in the desert one ends up eating sand instead of drinking water."

"When looking at volume of trade on an individual stock's chart, I always start with weekly charts. Once I see something on weekly charts, I confirm the signal on daily as well as monthly charts. If the same signals are visible on daily, weekly and monthly charts, then it follows that what I see is probably what is happening. The odds become quite low of my seeing something that is not there."

"Volume, however, is always relative. If a stock trades an average of 1 million shares a week, then suddenly it shows a big price jump to new highs along with a clearly visible jump in volume to 5 million shares or more during the week of the price jump, it is obvious to me that something has happened to create this increased interest in the stock. The volume explosion must be clear and without question. And at the same time, an already up trending stock must show a clear price jump accompanying the volume explosion. A signal like that is an indication to sit up and notice the stock. However, just because such a price and volume action is visible does not mean much. All the other factors we talked about earlier that apply to a new potential winning stock have to apply. The stock must be at or near all time highs. It must be a young stock that came to the market no longer than 10-15 years ago. The stock's 52 week high price must be at least twice its 52 week low price. The stock must show a clearly increasing volume on rising prices on its weekly charts. The picture must be complete. An incomplete picture does not offer enough conviction for me to test the waters."

"An almost certain signal of an up trending stock shows up on a weekly chart. One will clearly see prices rising on increased volume and the reactions or consolidations will be on average or less than average volume. This is a good sign."

"Interpreting price and volume action, however, requires a discerning eye. The art of learning to read such signals on a chart is a lot like reading an x-ray. It takes some time, practice and a lot of experience. Eventually, one is able to take a look at a chart and within seconds see many of the characteristics that jump out. Pretty much like a radiologist who can take a quick glance at an x-ray and immediately interpret some clearly visible signs. Once the initial signs are seen, at that point further careful study is needed."

"Sometimes I write in my commentary to my readers that interpreting the stock market goings on is hard to explain. I usually can identify and see a move coming but I find it hard to explain why I can identify the impending move. It is almost like the age-old definition of decency in free-speech. What is offensive language? It is hard to explain but one can recognize it when one sees it."

Once again, I picked up the sheet on which he was drawing his rough sketch. I have reproduced as figure 7, the rough sketch that Boyd scribbled down. I can clearly see the long months and years of consolidation on low uninteresting volume. In addition, as the stock makes it into all time new price high ground, I saw how Boyd had indicated increased volume. Finally at one point, the weekly volume just exploded as the stock entered new price highs on clearly well above any prior volume highs logged by the stock. I noticed he had scribbled with his hand a note that said, "Ideally this is the kind of stock that I like see. This one would make me sit up and start paying attention. What I have shown is a weekly chart spanning some years in time."

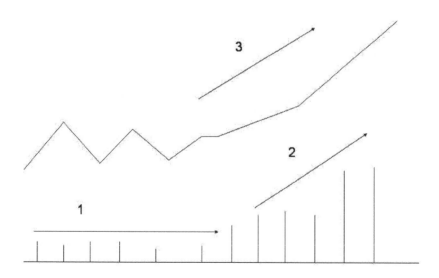

**Figure 7. An ideal price/volume action**

1 = long basing phase with quiet volume

2 = rising volume

3 = rising price accompanies rising volume

I noted with interest that he had written down a small note on the figure which said, "I may have to wait for months and months to see a set-up like this but the wait is usually well worth it."

At around this point Boyd glanced at his watch and noticed it was almost early evening. It had been a long day. So he decided to stop for the day. I gathered my notes and went home with some apprehension about finding a simplified but complete way to write down the day's lessons. I decided to include a handful of charts at some point within my writings to show typical price and volume action that shows up on potential winners. To simplify matters I decided to duplicate such annotated charts at the end after I was completely done with all the lessons.

## Summary:

Price and volume action should be complimentary. Volume must accompany prices in a way that there is little doubt of the impending and the ongoing move. Interpreting a stock's chart requires time, experience, repeated practice and a discerning eye. It takes three or four years of constant practice before one develops the skill for seeing things that can be seen on a stock's chart.

# CHAPTER 8
## BUY ONLY TRUE BREAKOUTS

The next morning at breakfast, Boyd was unusually low key and subdued. It was almost as if he was exasperated and exhausted by his efforts to show the winning ways to the public and hardly anyone listened. It was obvious to me that most folks could not follow the principles of success as expounded by Boyd because it required diligent, patient, careful and persistent navigation through the minefields of the stock market. The public at large wants instant action and results. We are a nation of instant gratification seekers and if we do not see instant results, then the approach must be flawed. With the enormous number of free-offers to the latest 'beat the market' gadgets, formulas, software, promises, gurus, who are eager to snag the gullible and offer the best get-rich-quick plan, the public has no use for the tried and true consistently winning plan and operation for market success. There are many back-tested results and model-portfolios that claim high triple digit gains year after year. The common man has no chance to make it in the market with so many vultures taking a piece of his account every time he blinks.

The market offers just enough crumbs for any and all systems of trading to keep the gullible coming back for more crumbs and along the way, the market takes huge chunks out of the gullible. The small crumbs are just enough to convince the gullible that their system has the chance to make it big, if only they can find the next big winner. Never once does it enter the minds of the gullible that big winners come along only 3 or 4 times during a 10-year cycle. To be able to trade successfully when such winners come along, the plan has to be safe and not to lose when times are bad. To achieve two goals diametrically opposed under the same umbrella of trading practices, one must devise a plan that works well in bad and good times.

The plan must be set on an auto-pilot so that the "human element" is eliminated and only the "winning element" is allowed to thrive. There was no other way to accomplish such a delicate balancing act than follow the principles that Boyd followed. There was nothing new in his over-all set of principles. There was, however, no other person alive who could implement and state the winning principles as Boyd could. There have been many greats, both known and unknown, who have followed and implemented such principles to extract millions from the markets. The unknown greats were probably better than the known greats. The known great operators included but were not limited to the likes of James Keene, Livermore, Baruch, John Gates, Russell Sage and Darvas. Boyd was one among the many unknown.

The over-all principle sounds easy enough - stay out of bad markets and be fully invested in good markets. The problem comes in implementing the plan. Many have hatched a great plan. Only a few could ever implement plans that confirmed the genius of the plan as it was hatched in principle. It is the same with the market. Words are plentiful. Cliches and adages are used left, right and center by the media and the know-it-all. The humility with which a genius executes the plan is truly a rare occurrence.

The term 'breakout' has received its share of bad press and good press. Bad press, thanks to folks who misuse its definition and do not know how to implement a true winning plan. Good press, from those who mainly offer a back-tested and a hindsight based claim to winning. In either case, the problem is the same. Too much media attention - which invariably only shows the extremes and fringes. The toughest work is done when no one is looking. The media only comes at the very end.

Boyd offered a simple definition of a breakout. A breakout is simply a move of a stock or an index from one price range to another. At its simplest level, it offers no clue as to the market's general direction or a stock's trend. For example, let us take a look at figure 8a. In this case, the stock price shown offers a breakout move. But there is no indication of whether the stock that made this breakout move is in any kind of a trend or not. There will be thousands of such breakouts in any given year, irrespective of the fact whether it is a good year or a bad year in the markets.

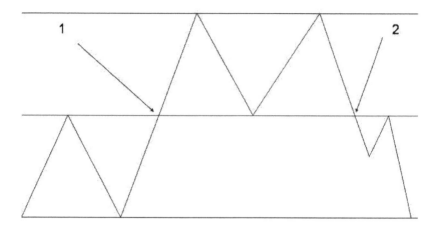

**Figure 8a. Any old breakout**

1 = a breakout from one price range to a higher price range

2 = return back to the original lower price range

On the other hand, let us consider figure 8b. Here we see a stock that has been building a long sideways base for years. And then, it suddenly wakes up and starts moving up. After moving up for some time, as measured in weeks and months, it settles down to base yet again. This second basing structure is, however, short and is measured in weeks. Thereafter, the stock breaks out to a higher price range.

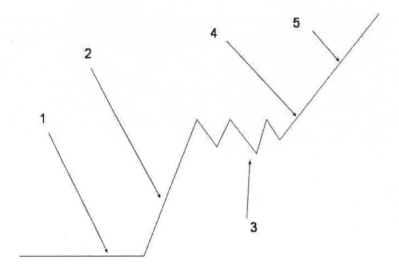

**Figure 8b. A true breakout**

1 = long sideways basing phase

2 = a strong up trend begun to make new price highs

3 = resting or consolidation phase

4 = breakout to new all time high price area

5 = continued up trend now resumed after the resting or consolidation phase

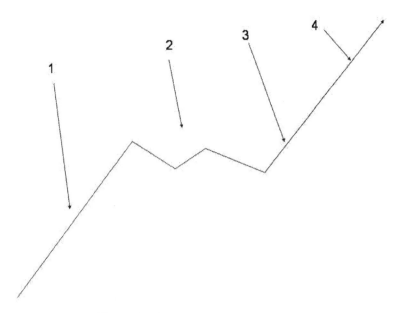

**Figure 8c. A close-up of a true breakout**

1 = a strong up trend begun to make new price highs

2 = resting or consolidation phase

3 = breakout to new all time high price area

4 = continued up trend now resumed after the resting or
consolidation phase

In order to show this picture up close, Boyd drew the same
figure, but with complete concentration now only on the prior
uptrend, the base and the breakout portion of figure 8b. This
figure is reproduced in figure 8c. Point 1 in this figure indicates
the prior uptrend. The prior uptrend confirms to us that the
stock has shown that it can rise in price. The area shown by
Point 2 is the basing area. This is the consolidation or the resting
phase where the stock takes a little break from its rising tendency.
Then at Point 3 a true break out occurs. A true breakout is when
a stock breaks into a new high price range after having met each
and every criteria below:

- the stock is less than 15 years old
- the stock has established a long period, as measured in years, of sideways basing pattern
- the stock then starts an uptrend by making it into new all-time price highs
- after showing an uptrend lasting many weeks and months, the stock then settles down into a consolidation, resting or basing phase

Boyd continued recounting his memories of his long gone younger days as he was covering the basics of breakouts. He said, "When I was a young man and new to the market, I made the mistake of trying to catch a move before the trend began. I used to think that I had to get in before the crowd got in. That is a mistake most folks continue to make in the market. This is the human element part of our downfall. It took me years and huge almost insurmountable losses to figure out that more money has been lost in trying to catch the bottom or the beginning of a move than anyone ever knew."

"It was after years and years of dealing with the market that I realized that I must be buying when the move has definitely begun and not one second before. I had to find a convincing signal that a serious move had begun. There is no point in anticipating a move. The move must have started with certainty before I should be buying. Anticipation of a move is another human failing that makes paupers out of most folks."

"It was when the light came on in my mind and I had realized that a move must be in progress before I should buy, that I realized the importance of defining a true breakout. It was then that I figured out the vast difference between a true breakout and the run-of-the-mill ordinary breakout."

I added, "I can see when the uptrend is evident on a stock. Obviously your rules and definition today have helped clarify it. However, for most folks it is hard to wait when they see a stock is moving up. The momentum guys will buy into a rising stock without waiting for a reaction. Upon the first sign of a reaction, the momentum players will dump the stock. How can you counteract this argument?"

Boyd replied, "It all depends on what is it you want out of the market. It is a lot like golfing. The machismo wants to show off the long drives off the tee. It is the finesse and the short game that makes the big bucks. If you want to show a drive here and there and get noticed for your drives, you will be one among the millions. But to be one among the millionaires, you have to have a great short game. If you want a few points here and there, by all means go ahead with momentum plays. But if you want the big bucks, you need the finesse and the patience to work with the stock and the market."

In addition to the definition of a true breakout and an up trending stock, Boyd covered a few of the confirming signals of a good stock. He continued, "A good stock is one which makes us money. Irrespective of how good a company is run or its products are, if one cannot make money on the stock, the stock is useless. Similarly, irrespective of how bad a company is run or how poor or unprofitable its products are, if the stock makes me money, then it is a good stock. The only good stock is a stock that makes me money. If a stock cannot make me money, then it is a lousy stock."

"Besides price and volume action, I also look for additional confirming signals. Like I said before, confirm everything. A trend does not begin in a vacuum. It takes time to finish a trend. It takes time to begin a trend. It takes time to change or reverse a trend. Therefore, every turning point has to be confirmed. Among some of the usual confirming signals include sister stock strength and index price/volume action."

I asked him to explain what he meant by a "sister stock." Boyd said, "If business is supposedly good for the entire home building and home construction business, it follows that all home building stocks must be doing well. Among the many homebuilding stocks, there will be one or two leaders who broke out first and began their up trends first. The rest of the home building stocks are sister stocks as they belong to the same industry as the two leading stocks. The one or two leaders will lead the group but the rest will follow and act as a confirming signal or sister stocks. I am wary when the group does not show strength among sister stocks. In the absence of sister stocks, we are either talking about a monopoly stock doing well in a group or one stock doing well in a weak group. If there is a monopoly stock doing well in a weak group, I might still be interested in the stock due to its monopoly type status. However, if there is no monopoly status and we see a leading stock in a weak group, I still am hesitant to consider such a stock as a potential buy."

After lunch, Boyd continued talking about price/volume action as he seemed to be baffled by the large resistance the general public had in keeping things simple. He was amazed that some glib talker with the latest gadgets and some new-found formula along with some technical jargon could sell his latest market beating secret to the public. Yet, the simplicity of making winning moves escaped the human mind. Even after decades of market action, Boyd was still confused by the human mentality. He could never understand the need each of us had to feel smart and superior to the market. The trap lay in the need to be superior and the need to feel smart. That need has been, is being and will be in the future exploited easily and with great success by the machinery in selling to the public a "new way to beat the market." In simple language, its is just another get-rich-quick scheme.

I broached the subject of fundamental analysis to Boyd. After the collapse of the internet and dotcom boom, earnings had suddenly become the "money" word. Nowadays, the brokers and the insiders would hype a good earnings report to help move a stock or help sell the stock to the public. Boyd said, "Yet again, I am impressed with the human element to help sink a stock trading account. Everything in the market is about the future. Nothing is about the present or the past. People buy stocks today to sell in the future at a higher price. In other words, the past has nothing to do with the future price of a stock. Nor does the present have anything to do with the price of a stock. Everything is about the anticipation of future growth. Past earnings growth has nothing to do with the future. It is only the anticipated earnings that matter."

It was getting late that afternoon. So I decided to throw in one last question, "You have said many times that price/volume action is all there is to know and that one must limit one's trades to no more than 5 or 7 trades a year. How can one accomplish such a task?"

Boyd was simple and clear in his response. He explained, "There have to be a set of rules that will keep me in good markets as long as the good conditions are in effect and not for a day longer. Similarly, the rules must keep me out of bad markets as long as bad conditions exist and not a day longer. Most importantly, the rules that keep me in good markets must also be the same ones that keep me out of bad markets. There cannot be two sets of rules - one for good markets and one for bad markets. It is impossible to have two sets of rules as they will become contradictory and more importantly, it is hard enough to stick to one set of rules, leave along two sets of rules."

"Why don't we cover the rules one by one in the coming days? However, to cut to the chase, the one simple way I try to limit my trades is by demanding unusual volume at breakout. What is unusual? I demand that my potential buy shows its average daily volume of trade of shares changing hands within the first hour of trade. Why? Well, by demanding such an unusually heavy volume, I am automatically limited to a handful of trades in any given year. I will discuss this more in the coming days."

## Summary:

Make sure the difference between a true breakout and a run-of-the-mill breakout is clear. Learn the basics of an up trending stock and its consolidation, resting or basing period. Learn your own human elements and place rules around you to stop the human elements from making decisions for you.

# CHAPTER 9
## CHART PATTERNS, SCHMATTERNS - WHO CARES?

The following morning as I drove up to Boyd's house and walked up to him pool-side, I noticed he had a stack of charts with him. While I considered myself an expert on charts, I knew enough about the market to know that I did not know it all. After exchanging greetings, I asked Boyd, "Is today all about charts?" He smiled and nodded and said, "As is typical about all things in the market, charting is about balance and confirmation. There is no single magic answer. However, it is definitely a giant piece of the puzzle. I am going re-visit some of the comments I made some days ago. I have learned that we humans have a very short memory. Repetition is the only cure to the human element in the market."

He continued, "It has long been a point of contention between those who rely on charts to read the market's message and others who look for economic indicators to see the market's direction - as to how much weight (if any) must be given to charts. I have been down both roads in the past few decades - and experience has time and again proven that 'proper chart interpretation' is invaluable. Besides learning from experience, it is clear to those of us who know a little something about the big boys that no single individual on this planet can out-do in research what the big boys do. Those who work on or near Wall Street know full well that the big boys have many many offices solely for research staff. The Goldmans, Lehmans, Bear Stearns of this world not only have many offices and many staffers but they have whole floors upon floors of research departments. There is no way in the world that any one of us individually can out do in research what these big guns do. They have the smartest, brightest, young and old, experienced, tech-savvy, chart-savvy and accounting minds splitting apart every balance sheet, studying every economic model, making every econometric projection, reading every chart, talking to every CEO of the stocks they follow, visiting the companies they study, doing market research on the competition and so on and so on. After all that work, investment in human talent and technological equipment, only about 10-15% of the big boys end up out-performing the market. While they have so many advantages, they have one major drawback in that when they make commitments, they have to build up the commitments over months and years. And when they liquidate their holdings, they have to do that over months and years. This is due to the large amount of funds they handle. Such funds cannot come in or out of stocks in one day or one week or one month. That one problem alone pretty much balances out their advantages and makes the playing field even for the individual speculators like us. Folks like us have the advantage in that we can sit in cash for as long as we desire or as long as the odds for wins are weak. We can get in and out easily without affecting the market."

"The biggest advantage we have is that we can 'see' what actions the big boys are taking after they have done all their exhaustive research. This we 'see' in the charts. This is one reason and a big reason alone that I have such a tremendous amount of conviction in the ability of a good chart reader. But like everything else, there are good chart readers and there are bad ones. The good ones will make sure that they are not seeing something that is not there. Bad ones will see what they wish to see rather than what is truly visible. That line is a fine line and one easily crossed even by the most experienced. The big boys have already done all the technical studies out there and they have even done studies that nobody knows and only the big boys' in-house technical staff does. After all those studies, then they act (buy, sell, hold, fold) and their actions will show up on charts - if only one knows how to read them correctly."

"Alright - you then ask - but the big boys read charts too. So they are reading what we are. And they are seeing what we are. Will they then not throw some red herrings to spoil the picture and to confuse folks like us? Of course, they will. Such red herrings are called 'fakeouts' or 'shakeouts.' But here is the thing....chart reading is one area where we can be better than the big boys. In addition, due to the way they have to build their positions and sell out their positions, the 'fakeouts' and 'shakeouts' will be minimal in good markets and plentiful in bad markets. Consequently, they end up confirming the market signals through their actions no matter what they do in no matter what market conditions."

"Remember the comparison I made of the market to a treasure hunt. Every participant has the same goal...to find the treasure. Every participant is given a set of clues to start the game. Some are better at deciphering the clues and moving from mile-post to mile-post. Every mile-post offers additional clues which will lead to the next mile-post if the clue is deciphered correctly. Along the way, some mile-posts have 'bad' or 'fake' clues which are red herrings. We know that red herrings are thrown down on a trail to confuse the dogs which follow scents. Similarly, these "fake" clues are offered to throw the participant off-track. Some participants are exceptionally smart and they figure out each and every clue correctly and discard the 'fake' clues and end up reaching the treasure first and quickest. These are extremely rare participants and there are not many like them. There is a second group of participants that is also very smart - though not as smart as the first group. This second group of participants deciphers some of the clues on their own but they tend to 'follow' the first group and thus are able to stick close to the first group. The first group knows that there is a second group 'following' them closely and thus the first group tries to throw in some 'shakeout' to try and throw the second group off-track. Eventually the second group reaches the treasure - although slightly behind the first group. These two groups take the biggest treasure. The rest of the participants range from mediocre, also-rans, somewhat lost to totally lost and clueless. We belong to the second group...since we 'follow' what the smart-money is doing by 'seeing' their actions on charts and through our own solving of some of the clues."

I knew Boyd to be a great chart reader. So I asked him to cover the basics and the essentials of chart reading. Like most market related skills, the biggest danger is always in trying to find a magic answer when one never exists. Chart reading skills are developed over years of reading charts over and over again. It is slow, boring and painful to the eyes. But of all the skills that can be developed, proper chart reading is one that is like learning to ride a bicycle. Once learned, the skill is never lost. One may get a little rusty if not constantly used. However, the rust wears away when one starts to practice again.

There are many books about charts and technical analysis out on the market. Some very good and most not so good. William Jiler's "How charts can help you in the stock market" is the best one out there which he wrote decades ago.

Boyd said, "I have seen some of the smartest folks lose their shorts in the markets because they have no respect for charts. There have been many who are so smart that the technical mumbo-jumbo like Elliot Wave, Fibonnacci numbers, MACD, Stochastics, Bollinger bands, etc. come easy to them and as a result have no respect for the simplicity of price/volume action. Such smart folks have lost their fortunes trusting some hyper-technical and cutting-edge scientific studies when the answer is always plain and simple and right in front of us. We humans have this uncanny ability and desire to complicate even the simplest of tasks. We do so because we have such a desire to prove to ourselves and to others that we are smarter than we are."

"Like everything else in the market, chart reading can be simplified or over-complicated. I believe in keeping things simple. I do not like to get confused. As soon as something starts to get my eyes to glaze over, I know I am in trouble. So I make it a point to keep everything as simple as possible. In reading charts, I get confused when I look at daily charts. Daily charts are too noisy. They show way too much volatility and add to the mixed messages. I rely solely on weekly charts. There is much more smoothness to weekly charts. Moreover, I do not have to pay much attention to all the jargon that chartists use like...cups, saucers, pennants, wedges, flags, head-and-shoulders, neck-lines, etc. They may or may not have their uses. Probably, the use is for the short-term scalpers. I am not a scalper. So these charting definitions do not apply to me. The only chart formation I pay attention to has been shown here."

At this juncture he drew the figure below which has been marked as Figure 9. It was the same figure as in Figure 8b but with volume being shown along with prices. The simplicity with which Boyd explained this chart surprised me. He pointed to the prior up trend and said, "This is an absolute essential to me. I must know for a fact that the stock has shown its ability to rise in price. Moreover, this ability to rise in prices must be on increased volume. This tells me that there is great buying interest in the stock. When a stock has such buying interest, odds are unlikely that it will get sold out. Once the up trend has stopped for a resting phase or the consolidation phase, volume must start to cool down. More the volume contraction, better the stock. When volume dies after a rising stock rises in price on volume, it tells me that all the buyers who bought during the rising phase are not willing to sell out. Low volume consolidation indicates higher prices to come with all the buyers having serious conviction of the stock's upward trend."

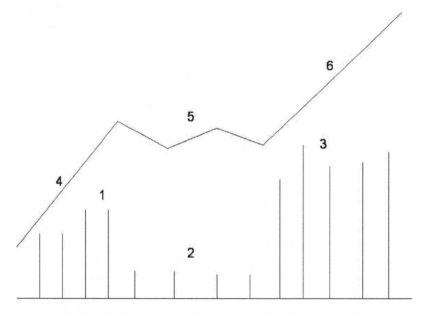

**Figure 9. A true breakout with solid price/volume action**

1 = rising volume during the prior up trend

2 = volume contraction during the resting or consolidating phase

3 = volume jumps to highest levels in the stock's all time history of trading volume

4 = prior up trend price area

5 = consolidation phase - the high price during this phase is a "ceiling" until the stock breaks above this "ceiling" price. Once it breaks above the "ceiling" price, then the "ceiling" becomes the "floor" price which is normally not penetrated to the down side again

6 = up trend resumes

"The tighter the price range during the consolidation the better. This adds to the conviction that nobody is willing to sell the stock. In a perfect stock, the consolidation price range would not exceed 10-20% and the volume would contract clearly with at least a week or two of volumes of trade that shrink well below 50% of normal weekly volume. And when the stock pierces its prior high on volume, it has psychologically cleared a ceiling or the upper resistance band. Once a true breakout like this occurs, this ceiling becomes the floor for the stock's price. A true breakout will never get below this floor price and it begins a truly successful up trend."

The chartists get confused and fall prey to the noise by paying too much attention to the shapes, patterns, pre-defined formations on daily charts. Daily charts are given to more false reading than are weekly charts. In addition, I do not want to define a pattern and fall prey to looking for signals on daily charts. The price/volume action during the prior uptrend and during the consolidation phase is far more important than the so-called pre-defined shapes and patterns that most chartists rely upon."

"I am not such a big fan of the cups, saucers, pennants and flags that many die-hard chartists use. I see the picture my way. Everybody sees the same picture in different ways. By using patterns and formations to define a chart, even the most experienced chartists will see a picture with a bias. I wish to avoid the bias. Therefore, I rely on the simplest forms of interpretation of the chart. Which is purely price and volume action on weekly charts."

I thought this was way too simplistic. I mentioned this to Boyd. His answer was simple. He said, "That is the whole point. I do not ever want to see something that is not there. In order to do that I must keep things at the simplest level. This will ensure that I will not fall for the numerous traps that the market will lay for me."

## Summary:

Pay attention to the price and volume action on weekly charts. Try and make sure that one does not see what is not there. The bias in seeing what one wishes to see is far more prevalent than one will ever know. Learn chart interpretation through practice. A stock must show volume during its rising phase to prove that buying interest is large. A stock should consolidate or rest on low volume to confirm that selling interest is non-existent. A break out to new highs must come about on unusual volume.

# CHAPTER 10
## BREAKAWAYS ARE GOOD BETS

While Boyd was not too keen on expounding on the so-called definitions of specific patterns and was more interested in showing the generalities of charts, he did mention that true breakaway patterns are solid bets. A breakaway, by definition, is a stock that breaks out with extremely heavy volume. A breakaway stock shows usually the heaviest one day volume in its history as it makes into brand new all time highs. Such a move is amplified due to volume explosion as the stock gaps up into new price high area. A gap up is a price area which is "skipped over" by a stock due to tremendous buying demand. A simple breakaway is shown in figure 10 below.

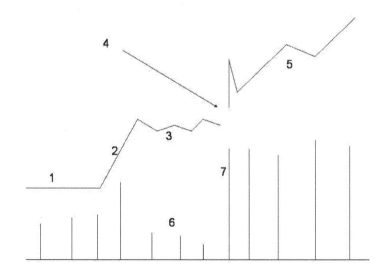

Figure 10. A true breakaway

1 = long sideways basing phase

2 = a strong up trend begun to make new price highs

3 = resting or consolidation phase

4 = breakaway gap

5 = continued up trend now resumed after the resting or consolidation phase

6 = dead volume during resting phase

7 = highest volume of trade shown in the stock's all time trading history

The prior long basing pattern and the subsequent uptrend are clear enough to see and understand since prior lessons addressed these matters. It is the break out point that is uniquely different in breakaways. In the example shown, one will note that the volume of shares traded on the day of the breakaway is the stock's highest one day volume of trade ever. The price itself gaps up to new high price area. The stock gaps up when it closes the day prior at a price that is well within the basing price range. However, the breakaway day opening price is well above the basing area and usually (but not always), the opening price is near the low price for the day of the breakaway. Explosive volume accompanies the breakaway as the stock usually trades easily six-to-ten or more times its average daily volume. Even more remarkable is the confirmation shown on weekly charts of the stock as the weekly volume of trade will also be the highest weekly volume in the stock's all-time trading history.

However, like all true winning stocks, trading a breakaway effectively is somewhat tricky. Sometimes, the breakaway may test prices as much as 10% below the low of the breakaway day. Which means, a standard 10% stop-loss may be taken out many times before the true up trend begins. On breakaways, therefore, Boyd would allow as much as 15% stop-loss price below the buy price. Since the first entry would be minimal in dollar amounts, the test-buy would be allowed the extra leeway just because the odds of a truly big move were so much higher on true breakaways.

Like everything else in the stock market, it also required a serious speculator to maintain the detachment and consider each breakaway on its own individual merit. It also required one to be very specific about the definition of a breakaway. Not every gap nor every huge volume explosion was a breakaway. A breakaway is unique and the only definition is as shown in figure 10. It is paramount, as Boyd used to say, to not to ever see something that is not there.

In addition, a breakaway does not make its big move in one day or one week. It takes months to make the true move. How effectively and successfully one trades it and how successfully one is able to pyramid on it would dictate the returns on such potentially explosive moves.

## Summary:

Breakaways are solid bets if they come about early on, just before or just after a true market up trend has begun. If one can trade breakaways effectively, very few other trades will be needed during any given market cycle to outperform the major indices handily. Though breakaways are solid bets, learning to trade them correctly is very important. Breakaways toward the end of a market cycle usually signify a topping stock. Care must be taken to interpret where the market cycle is, before considering large commitments into a breakaway stock.

# Chapter 11
## Rules of Speculation and the Basics

There are more than tens and hundreds of services out on the market that tout to have a special program that beats the market. They all claim to have arrived to such a claim by "back-testing." Back-testing is nothing but a gimmick to show huge returns. Back-testing means tweaking the buy-sell points and programs to "fit" a move of a stock or a group of stocks who have already finished their moves. What the common man does not understand is that one can come up with any program and find a set of stocks that will "fit" the program after-the-fact. It is a given that no such programs offer such moves before-the-fact and nor do they ever show a winning stock "during" the move.

If one just thought about the obvious, it would strike us plainly that if such a successful program existed, the program-maker would make his killing in the markets using his program instead of trying to market his program to the public.

However, as Boyd had explained in one of his earliest lessons, as long as we keep searching for the magic answer that beats the market all the time we are bound to keep losing. Sooner the reality sinks in that beating the market takes time, hard-work, discipline, patience and many years of learning, sooner we can start preparing ourselves to tackle the smartest thing that exists - which is the market.

Besides all the numerous lessons that we must learn to be successful at speculating, one of the most important ones is the lesson on money management. Money management is as important a technique as any of the other important techniques in making solid gains in a good market and keeping out of trouble in bad markets. It is also one of the hardest lessons to get the hang of. The biggest obstacles in learning money management principles are the usual culprits - greed, fear, hope, over-confidence, arrogance, wishful-thinking, lack-of-confidence and despair. The good thing about these huge obstacles is that they are all human failings. While overcoming human failings pose great challenges, it also makes it possible to overcome these failings with a set of rules. The rules are always in place to avoid human mistakes.

The market operator should first and foremost accept the fact that there are only two elements in the market. One is the "winning element" and the other is the "human element." It is obvious to most of us that all the major losses one experiences in the market place is due to the "human element." Similarly, all the major wins in the market come about due to the "winning element." As Boyd continued explaining the workings of a successful speculator, I mentioned to him that I need some clarifications of the terms "the winning element" and "the human element."

As was usual, his explanations were simple. The simple answer is that "the winning element" is that part of a speculator's operation that leads to major wins in good markets, minor wins in mediocre markets and to minor or no losses in bad markets. The simple explanation of "the human element" is that part of a novice operator's actions that lead to minor gains in good markets, big losses in mediocre markets and total devastation in bad markets.

The market can offer only one of five outcomes - major wins, minor wins, breakeven, minor losses or major losses. The "winning element" is responsible for major wins, minor wins, breakeven and minor losses. The "human element" is responsible for minor wins and major losses. Since there are only two elements in the market place, it becomes paramount that we concentrate on learning all that we can about both the "winning elements" and the "human elements." Then we must learn to accept and execute all that we can about "the winning elements." At the same time we must learn and avoid at all costs executing all that we can about "the human element."

In this day and age of computers and software, there is a big myth and a large misguided segment of the market participants which thinks that a program or a software is an answer to avoiding the "human element." Software and programs are just another hook by the Wall Street machinery to sell to us gullible folks the magic answer to beating the market. There are no magic answers. The answers truly lie within each one of us. We must know all we can about ourselves and learn about all our weaknesses and strengths as humans. Once we know who we are and what our personality is, then we can implement and follow a set of rules that will keep us out of trouble in bad times and keep us fully in positions in good times.

Boyd went on to say that the rules he followed and the rules he advocated to his readers worked for him and for folks who had personalities like his. I asked him to elaborate how he would describe his personality. Yet again his words were simple and straight to the point. He said that he was a speculator and he would be interested in placing his money only when winning big had a good probability. He would place small amounts in the market to first prove that his take of the market was right. If he started making money on his small test buys, he would then start adding to his positions carefully always making sure that he would place trailing sell-stops to ensure he would never lose on a winning stock. If the test buys showed losses after losses by hitting his stop-loss prices, he would stay out of the market until he could see that conditions had improved. He never wanted to give back to the market any more than just an insignificant amount from what he extracted from the market. And most of all, he never relied on anyone else but himself. He would start always with the assumption that the market is bad. It was then up to the market to prove him wrong and convince him that the good market was here to stay before he could place large amount of funds in his positions.

It was then that Boyd started getting into his rules of speculation. Before I realized it he was already talking about his first rule of "do no harm." Even though he had covered the terms before, he now went into his rules step by step.

## First Rule of Speculation - First, Do No Harm

While saying "first, do no harm," is easy enough, implementing and executing the rule is hard for most novices. Experienced operators see this as second nature and it comes about without a second's thought. We had covered in prior lessons that the normal first time market participant or any market participant, for that matter, comes with a huge telegraphed message when he or she looks to the market for riches. The message is telegraphed to all the vultures out there that a new source of capital has arrived into the market. The vultures are hovering above us trying to look for the next piece of meat to be devoured. As soon as the message comes to the vultures that a new piece of meat is coming, the descent is swift and the attack is quick.

As soon as an account is opened by a participant, he or she suddenly is offered all kinds of information - good, bad and indifferent. The overload of information is vast. The noise and the distraction created is immense. The decision to spend the trading capital is made, pushed, hyped, encouraged and coerced in various forms ranging from the subtle to the overbearing pressure. With such a bombardment of information, the participant has very little chance to survive the onslaught by the vultures.

Boyd said that the first test for most new entrants is to control themselves and see if they can withstand at least a period of three months without ever buying anything. If they can survive a three month period without spending a dime of their trading capital, they may have a chance of outperforming the market.

Successful speculation is not easy and it requires a very special mentality. Such a mentality does not exist among the common folks. Since it is a given that more than 80% of the folks who come to the market will lose over the longer-term, the vultures have no mercy. They will pluck away at the trading account until nothing is left. When there is only one out of every five who can come ahead at the end of any 10-year cycle, the vultures have no incentive to warn the prey of impending doom. In the land of the merciless, the vulture who dares to warn the prey goes hungry.

In the long history of the stock market, almost everybody has made some money on some stock at some time or another. That is not the test, though that is the memory. It is a fact that most will give back more to the market than they will ever take out from the market. However, that is not the memory as most will not remember their losses. Most will remember the rare one win and using that as the gauge will endeavor to repeat that win despite numerous losses along the way that prove such wins are rare to come by. It is a beautiful trap orchestrated by the market to offer crumbs in temptation and thus, setting up the sting that will kill most accounts.

Nobody ever advises a buyer not to buy. That is fool-hardy since the buyer has already telegraphed his intention to buy irrespective of what the conditions are. He has opened a trading account and has already fished for some information about "what is a good buy?" That is a giant flashing sign to the vultures which says, "Here I am. Come and get me. The one who gets me first gets the biggest bite." Once the bias has set in that the market is a buy, the market participant has very little chance of escaping unscathed unless, of course, a wild bull market is in place. In a wild bull market even the worst stocks move up. It would be very hard to lose in a wild bull market. A wild bull market, by definition, is a market that is bubble like and all stock prices seem to move up.

## Second Rule of Speculation - Check-off Your Check List Before Buying

Boyd came back to the basics he had covered in prior lessons. And he put together a small check-list that he would mark off to confirm that the market was right to place his test-buys. He listed his check-list as follows:

- Is the general market in an up trend?

To confirm that the market was indeed in an up trend, Boyd would use weekly charts to see that the Dow, the S&P500, the Nasdaq and the Transports would not conflict with "higher highs and higher lows." If indeed the market was in an up trend or looked to be beginning an up trend, he would check off this point on his list.

- Do I see any 20/4 type stock movements?

As covered in prior lessons, a 20/4 type move in Boyd's definition was a stock that broke out to new high prices on volume after consolidating for some weeks and then making at least a 20% move from its breakout price within 4 weeks. He would add an additional requirement that all 20/4 type moves should never get below their buy-price pegged as the last high of the consolidation phase.

- Do I see price and volume action that confirms everything I see?

Besides the indices showing signs of an up trend, their volume action should confirm that buying is coming with increased volume. A similar confirmation must be available on the leading 20/4 type stocks as well.

## Third Rule of Speculation - If I cannot make money on test-buys, I cannot make money on large funds

I had learned early on that the amount of trading capital does not dictate success. If I cannot make money on a small percentage of my trading capital, I cannot make money on a larger percentage of my capital. In other words, if I am not right about the market's trend and my stock's trend, it does not matter whether I put $10,000 or $1 million in the stock, I will still take a loss.

A smart speculator first observes the market events. If the market seems to be logging higher highs and higher lows with volume confirmation, he then looks for leading individual stocks for additional signs. If the leading individual stocks confirm the market's action, he then tests the market and the stock to confirm if what he is seeing is what is actually occurring. This test-buy is usually a very small amount from his over-all trading capital. Boyd used anywhere from 5-10% of his trading capital as his test buy amount. The test-buy is one way to overcome the hurdle of "the wish should not be allowed to become the father of the thought." In just wishing for a bull market, one should not see a non-existing bull trend. The test-buys will confirm or deny the market's trend. If the test-buy starts to make money, then and only then can one contemplate placing incrementally larger and larger funds into the market.

## Fourth Rule of Speculation - Always use a stop-loss in place to protect the account from oneself

A stop-loss is a pre-determined maximum amount of loss one is willing to accept on any one trade. This is simple enough for most experienced speculators to understand and implement. Boyd used a 10% stop-loss and others use a different amount. The idea of a pre-determined stop-loss is to avoid becoming what Livermore used to call "an involuntary holder of stock." If a stock was bought at $50 per share and after some days and weeks it fell to $45 per share, the stock is worth $45. If one holds the stock "hoping it will come back," then one is 'involuntarily" holding the stock. The trader really does not want this stock that is moving down in price but is holding it despite his distaste for the stock only with hopes of it coming back to his breakeven price. What if the stock continues down and goes to $40? And if a few days later the stock hits $35 price. Then what? Again, the typical participant would continue holding the stock "involuntarily" hoping the price will come back. All major losses in the market start off slowly and insignificantly. By the time the small losses have ballooned into large losses, it is usually too late to rectify the damage.

The stop-loss is a mechanism that tells a speculator that he is wrong. If he is wrong about the market's direction and/or about a stock's direction, the only way he knows that is when the stock or the market starts to move against him. If the stop-loss price gets hit and the speculator is taken out of the market, it is the market sending him a message that his original market outlook was likely wrong. If such a stop-loss is not in place, it is very easy to talk ourselves out of selling out when we should sell out. We need protection from ourselves as we will be the main cause for the market beating us. This is the insurance policy against the "human element" that was discussed earlier.

The only reason we buy stocks is to make money on its rising prices. If the stock does not rise in price, there is no need to buy the stock. If the stock rises in price, then no other signal is needed as the stock is proving to us through its rising prices that we are right. If we are right on a small test-buy, then we are very likely going to be right on larger amounts of funds. Thus, once the test-buys make gains, we are prepared to place larger funds in the market with more confidence.

## Fifth Rule of Speculation - The trend is your friend and move your stops along the trending move

Some of the points Boyd made sounded repetitious but I was smart enough to recognize that on the surface what seemed repetition was in fact adding more clarity to the points and the principles of successful speculation. An up trend is, by definition, a series of price movements where higher highs and higher lows were pegged.

The basic principle of successful speculation is to never sell a rising stock and to never buy a stock that is not rising in price. An additional extension of this principle is to sell a stock which is not rising. But the balancing act required of holding a rising stock just long enough until its movement upwards continues and then at the same to sell a stock which has stopped rising further is an extremely tricky one. More money has been lost and more paupers have been created in chasing the bottom or the top of a move. Catching tops and bottoms are almost impossible. If one catches the top or the bottom of a move, it is by chance or by luck or a combination of both.

Baruch, a well-known speculator of his time, used to say that only liars caught the top or the bottom of a move consistently. A true speculator has to accomplish the task of riding a rising stock for as long as possible and at the same time he has to sell out before the stock starts reversing and starts its move downward. In addition, making big money takes time in the markets. Time is relative as we all know. In the United States an hour is a long time. In Tibet, a few years is considered a short time. However, it has been seen time and time again that the best and the fastest movements in a rising stock occurs between 4-8 month periods of time. Beyond the 8-month mark, usually a reaction of significant proportion takes away a good segment of the gains made during the prior up trend.

How to accomplish this contradictory set of goals? One, to hold the stock as long as possible and through minor or intermediate reactions. Second, to sell-out close enough to the top of a significant move and before a significant retracement in price begins.

Boyd said that it is hardest to keep things simplest. His rule was to keep moving his sell-stops a little below a rising stock's last low before the new high. His belief was that weekly price moves were more reliable than daily price history. As an example, he referred to his sketch as shown in Figure 11.

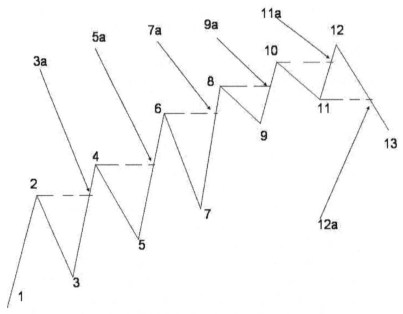

**Figure 11. Moving stops along a trending move**

Boyd said, "Assume you own a stock that is rising in price. I have drawn a sketch of such a stock. Let us say you bought the stock as it cleared the point 3a when it made new price highs. As soon as you get bought in at 3a, you would place a sell-stop at 10% below the price at 3a. Assume that the sell-stop price is not touched until the stock has logged a higher high and a higher low. This means the stock has to first log a high price at point 4. Then its reaction to this move up must be pegged, such as it is at a price at point 5. Note that the price at point 5 is higher than the price at point 3 - the stock's last low. Then the stock has to log a new higher high, such as it does at a price at point 6. Note that the price at point 6 is higher than its prior high price at point 4. During the course of the stock price's move from point 5 to a price at point 7, it passes through or pierces above the price at 5a which is essentially the same price as logged as a high at point 4. As soon as the stock pierces above this point 5a, the stock has now re-confirmed its up trend. It is at this point in time that the sell-stop is moved from the prior sell-stop to a little below the price at point 5."

"The sell-stop remains at a little below the price at point 5 until another round of higher highs and higher lows have been confirmed. This means the stock has to first log the high as indicated by the price at point 6. The stock must then react to this new high price at point 6. The reaction is shown to be pegging a low price at point 7. Then a new leg of upward move begins. During this new move up from the price at point 7 to the price at point 8, the stock must pierce or pass through the price high pegged at point 6. I have indicated this price to be a price at point 7a. As soon as the stock moves past this price at 7a, I then move my sell-stop from a little below the price at point 5 to a little below the price at point 7. The sell-stop placed now at a little below the price at point 7 is not moved until yet another complete round of higher highs and higher lows are pegged."

"On paper this seems quite simple and straight-forward enough. The biggest hurdle most novices face is that they pay attention to their account values and to their stock prices day in day out. When they see the stock has pegged a high at, for example, point 6 and then they see it react to the price at point 7, they start getting nervous. They feel that they are 'losing' their profit and the novice will sell out at the first hint of price weakness."

"The discipline to follow sell-stops along the trending move takes time to develop. Most folks get the hang of this discipline only after "missing out" on the big wins. It is only after many have let go of a true winner very early in the trend many many times, that many folks will get the hang of trading along the trend. Regrettably, many others will never get the grasp of the simplicity of the discipline. Like I said, time is relative. Four to eight months is not a long period of time in the stock market for people like me who have seen and experienced the gifts and the dangers of the market for decades. But for novices and many undisciplined professionals (who will not remain professionals for long), even 4-8 weeks seem like an eternity."

And he continued, "As the stock keeps making these higher highs and higher lows, the stops keep moving up along the trending move. At some point the upward price pressure will stop. And then the pressure starts to build to push the prices down. The turn comes with subtlety some times and at other times it comes with complete clarity. But the speculator who keeps his rules in place will keep moving his stops up. First the stop moves to a little below the price at point 9. Then to a little below the price at point 11. As the stock tops out for the intermediate or longer term and starts to head down, this stop will get hit and the stock is sold out. The speculator was thus able to ride with the stock from a price at point 3a to the price at point 11. That is a significant move and that is the true goal of a sharp speculator - to grab and ride the meaty or the significant part of a trending move."

## Summary:

Follow the rules of successful speculation. First, do no harm. Before buying anything, check-off the check list for buying and confirm that the conditions are ripe for buying. If money cannot be made on small test buys, then money cannot be made on larger funds. Follow the trend. Have a pre-determined risk that you are willing to take on each position. Place a sell-stop at your risk level to ensure that the position is liquidated should your risk level be touched off. Keep moving your stops up along the trending move.

# CHAPTER 12
## ADDITIONAL RULES OF SPECULATION AND THE BASICS

Almost no one talks about proper money management while speculating. If one walked into a broker's office and opened an account for stock trading, it is a given that ten times out of ten, the broker will recommend a buy immediately. Besides recommending a buy, nine times out of ten the broker will recommend spending all the capital that is available in the trading account.

The same scenario plays out even when a novice or an undisciplined professional (who uses other folks' money to play in the stock market) starts to trade in the market. Almost immediately upon opening an account buys are made. In most cases, all the available capital is exhausted in purchases of stock within the first 48 hours of the account being open.

The classic speculator, on the other hand, never ever shows his entire hand. He never ever places his commitments where he uses all of his capital from the get go. The shrewd speculator always allows for the fact that he must be proven right first, before any additional or large commitments can be made in the market.

Even the terminology used by speculators is different and unique to successful operators. Only a speculator will call himself a speculator. A true speculator will never call himself a trader, a gambler, an investor or a long-term investor. Similarly, a gambler will never call himself a gambler. The speculator and the gambler are on either side of the spectrum. Over a full life-time, the speculator comes out ahead in the market as he takes out more from the market than he gives to the market. The gambler on the other hand gives it all back to the market and never takes anything out. The trader gives and takes but hardly ever is able to take large sums out. The investor also gives and takes and usually gives large sums to the market.

As Boyd had discussed, a speculator only lays out his commitments when odds of wins favor him. The gambler lays out his plays without any regard to the odds of wins. The trader tries to scalp a few points here and a few points there. The investor sits through long cycles of bull and bear trends and gives up more during bear trends than he ever made during bull trends.

Chief among the terminology that a true speculator uses is the term "commitment." The very word offers visions of "gripping" or "holding on to" something worth having. It also offers visions of "sitting through good days and bad days." A commitment is to a speculator the key to success. A commitment to the rules. A commitment to the system of market operation. A commitment to discipline. A commitment to sit out if conditions so dictate. A commitment to stick with a position as long as the conditions dictate. And so on. Until the rules, the stock or the market in some confirming way do not offer a clear change of position, the speculator will stay committed to the position he has taken.

## Sixth Rule of Speculation: I must start making gains on my positions from Day One and within four weeks the stock must have made at least 20% move from my buy price to its high-price

Most of the big gains that one makes start off with a bang. There are occasional slow beginners - but by and large, the majority of the big movers start the move from day one. As soon as the first step of market entry is made on a test-buy, the sell-stop is immediately placed below the buy price - usually at 10% or so below one's buy price. The stock is then given time to either prove or disprove its mettle. The stock can only do one of three things - it can go up, it can go down or it can go nowhere.

We have an action that needs to be taken, based on each of these three scenarios. If the stock moves up, it must move at least 20% or so from its buy-price to the most recent high price within four weeks of a purchase. If four weeks have passed and our stock has not come close to the 20% move from its buy price level, we must be prepared to start looking at other prospects and be willing to let go of our first stock. On the other hand, if the stock starts to move down instead of moving up, then it will trigger the sell-stop and will eliminate us from the market.

Let us assume the stock makes the 20/4 type move that we have as our first target. Then the sell-stop must be moved immediately from its then current level to a new price of "a little above the buy price." This will ensure that one never takes a loss on any 20/4 type stock. Once the first stock has reached this point where the worst case scenario is that we will breakeven on the position, it is only then that we should consider taking a second position. In other words, never buy a second stock unless the first stock has a sell-stop that will, at worst, offer a breakeven trade.

Once a 20/4 type stock has been collected, it must from that point onwards continue its up trend. The up trend must be clearly visible on weekly charts. On weekly charts, an uptrend manifests itself as a series of higher highs and higher lows. As the stock keeps making this series of higher highs and higher lows, the sell-stops must be kept moving up to a "a little below the last low." The moving sell-stop was discussed in a prior lesson.

## Seventh Rule of Speculation: Do Not Buy a Second Stock Unless the First Stock has Made a Gain

Boyd was a classic. I had never seen anyone like him. He would say time and again that everybody makes rules but hardly anyone follows them. This is what separated the successful speculator from the public. He would always say that the public would change the rules to suit the day. In other words, based on the person's bias of the day, he or she would change the rules to fit the bias.

The one advantage Boyd had over most others was that he had been broken by the market completely. It was an advantage because that cruel experience had taught him to never to take the market lightly. As it turns out, most very successful speculators learn their lessons the hard way. Most who come back to the market to avenge the huge losses, do so with great patience and with complete awareness of the market's ability to kill most accounts.

Boyd would use the classic line, "Never take a second step forward until you make sure you are on firm ground with your first step." Every move he made forward in the market would be completely dictated by the outcome of his previous step.

Having first ensured that his first test-buy made a 20/4 type move, he would then move the sell-stop on that position to a little above his buy-price. This would ensure that he never took a loss on any 20/4 type mover. This was the rule to keep him focused completely on only those stocks that showed the ability to move from the get go. Once he found such a stock, he would make sure that he never took a loss on such a stock to imprint on his psyche that he can always "stick with" the 20/4 movers since they never showed him a loss. It was the "sticking with" the winners that made the big bucks.

Once this first step had been taken, where a 20/4 mover's sell-stop had been moved to a little above the breakeven price, only then would Boyd start to consider a second entry. There was no sense buying a second stock when the first stock had not clearly shown the juice. It was only after the first step proved to be right, that a second step could be contemplated.

Boyd was a firm believer that "life in the market was a cinch inch by inch and hard by the yard." It is when folks want to make 300% return in days and weeks when it takes months and years that failure is guaranteed. Everything in the market takes time and patience. To make sure that time and patience work hand in hand, the rules have to be devised and implemented.

## Eighth Rule of Speculation: Pyramid Only When Odds are Working in your favor and Make Sure the Pyramid Buy Will Never Result in a Loss on the Over-all Trade

Pyramiding involved buying a second and/or a third position on a stock that one already owned. For example, if one bought a stock when it broke out to new highs at a price of $30, and some weeks and months later, it offered a chance to buy at a higher price as it broke out of a higher consolidation at a price of $45, then the second buy would be called a pyramid buy.

Boyd would keep everything he did simple. For example, when I asked him, "Assume we talk about this stock that offered a first test-buy at $30 price and then offered a pyramid buy at a $45 price, how much additional stock would I be buying at the $45 price?"

In keeping with his "simplicity is best" rule in the markets, he offered the example with some dollar figures. He said, "Assume you bought 200 shares at $30 price as the test-buy. Let us assume you placed a sell-stop at $27 promptly upon buying your test-buy. This is your 10% below the buy as the stop-loss . Let us then assume the stock ran to $36 within 3 weeks and thus qualified to be a 20/4 type mover. As soon as the stock hit the $36 price level, you moved your sell-stop from $27 to $30.50. Now after some weeks the stock hits a high price of $45 and then reacts and consolidates between $45 and $39 price level. Once this consolidation phase is complete, let us say the stock breaks out to new highs above $45. This is when you are buying your pyramid buy. 10% below the $45 price would be the normal stop-loss or $40.50 would be the next stop-loss price if I bought the pyramid buy at $45. To calculate the amount I would buy at $45, I take the 200 shares I bought at $30 and figure that I have a gain of $2100 at the $40.50 new sell-stop price level. This is the maximum I am willing to lose should the second buy or the pyramid buy start to go against me. Which means the maximum total I can buy is $2100 divided by $4.5 per share that I would lose if my new sell-stop got hit. This works out to be 466 shares. I would never buy more than 466 shares as the pyramid buy amount at the $45 price level."

I now saw that he was making sure that he never took a loss on a winning stock. Even in the worst case scenario, had the stock fallen back from its new pyramid buy price of $45 to down to $40.50 and triggered his sell-stop, he would never have taken any loss on the stock. Boyd's rule of "never take a loss on a winning stock" became clearer to me.

I asked Boyd about how many times can one pyramid. He said that he almost never bought more than two times. In most cases he would stop after the second buy unless the third buy was possible and clearly visible on a very strong up trending stock in a bull market. He said, "Rare exceptions like Taser do show up during a confirmed bull trend when a third buy is clearly possible."

## Ninth Rule of Speculation: If Many Leading 20/4 Type Stocks Start Hitting Their Sell-stops, the Market Maybe Showing Signs of Danger

Every cycle would bring with it a new batch of leading stocks. Some times a stock may be a leader for two consecutive cycles in the market. However, it would be highly unusual to see the same stock be a leader for more than two cycles. The reason was quite simple - once a stock was fully distributed into the public's hands, there was no more any need for the insiders to run up the stock's price. Since the stock being distributed into the public's hands meant that the insiders were no longer the insiders, they had no more need to work the prices up. In other words, its leadership role had been fulfilled.

This was one reason why Boyd would never look beyond the most recent 15 years of data to look for new leaders. It was obvious that a stock that had been in existence for more than 15 years had plenty of prior cycles and "good economic times" to make their moves. Once such stocks made their moves, they had offered plenty of opportunities for the insiders to have sold out of the stock. Since such insiders were no longer holders of the stock, they had very little incentive to let the stock make a big run. If a stock had no incentive to make a big run, there was little chance to be able to make solid gains off such a stock. If making gains was not possible, why buy into such a stock?

The market is full of risk. To compensate for the risk, it must offer stocks that can double one's money during any given cycle. If stocks that truly have the potential and the desire to double in prices in a given cycle are not showing up, why bother participating in the market.

**Tenth Rule of Speculation: Do not look to make any gains in bad markets. It is better to stay out of bad markets where odds of wins are against us, rather than trying to swim against the tide.**

Once the leading stocks start to hit their sell-stops, it is but a matter of time before most, if not all, get sold out. The sell decision is best left to sell-stops to activate. When the general market is in a down trend or in a trend less and a choppy form, the prospects of making any tradable gains are small. With the larger view of "first, do no harm," it would be a grave mistake to give back any portion of the hard earned gains. The gains made were hard and achieved through extreme patience, hard work and discipline. It is easy to give back the hard-earned gains during bad market conditions. It is far better to protect the gains made by not getting involved promptly in any potential new rally. The new rally can only be confirmed by the action of leading stocks. The lessons have already been learned in prior chapters about fixing the beginning of a reliable rally. The beginning of a down trend is signaled by the sell-stop getting hit on many of the leading stocks. In addition, a confirmation will be evident on the leading indices such as the Dow Industrials, the S&P500, the Nasdaq and the Dow Transports. The down trend is, by definition, a series of lower highs and lower lows. The beginning is usually indicated by volume selling early on. The recovery from the volume selling is usually on weaker volume and the recovery never gets to the prior highs. Well before the indices confirm a dangerous market, leading stocks would have given clear indications when they hit their sell-stops. As we have learned from prior lessons, we would have placed sell-stops at a little below the prior low on up trending stocks. By taking out a prior low, an up trending stock negates its uptrend.

**Eleventh Rule of Speculation: If the best stocks are not moving up in price, the market has no chance of offering good odds of wins. If the best stocks are moving up in price, no other reason is needed to be buying and if the best stocks are not moving up in price, no other reason is needed to avoid buying.**

As simple as this sounds, following the rule is hard. It is inbuilt in us humans to find a gem that no other human has found. We want to be the first to get to the treasure before everybody else gets there. The game of treasure hunt is always on. The problem is that in bad market conditions, the number of false clues are amplified. In addition, the Wall Street machinery must keep the wheel turning by continual hype to keep the public on a buying spree. The "buy the bargain" and every 'sale' is a good bargain is the American consumer's mentality which is exploited to the fullest.

At every reaction on the way down, the drum-beat of "this is the beginning of a new bull market" is sounded off. Nobody wants to miss out on making money. Making money is the modern day equivalent of the cave-man's ability to hunt, kill and bring home the bacon. Every human has seen at least one win during their lifetime. That one win is stored in the memory banks in all of us. That one win is in many ways a lure to get hooked on every subsequent trap laid by the market. At every step after that one big win, the "human element" in us believes, rightly or wrongly, that the next such big win is right around the corner. The chase for such a big winner is never ending despite lousy odds of wins in the market.

We are smart folks. But the smarter we are, usually more stubborn we are in the belief that the market can be beaten handily and easily. After all, we are gifted with superior intellect. There is, however, no other entity with better intellect than the market. The sooner we accept this, the faster we will learn the basics of successful speculation.

## Summary:

The true winners start making gains from day one. Usually, the best movers qualify to be 20/4 type movers without ever hitting the sell-stop placed by the speculator. Do not buy a second stock until the first stock has made gains. Pyramid only when the odds of wins are in your favor and when the pyramid buy's worst case scenario will never make you take a loss on the over-all trade. If many 20/4 type stocks start hitting their sell-stops, the market may be indicating impending danger. In bad conditions, do not look to make gains rather look to avoid losses. If the best stocks are not making money, the market has no chance in offering good odds of wins.

# CHAPTER 13
## MORE RULES OF SPECULATION AND THE BASICS

I was getting a little concerned that the rules were adding up one by one and turning out to be too many to keep track of. I brought it to Boyd's attention. He responded with, "Do not worry. At the end of our lessons, I will summarize all the rules in a much simpler form. It will become very easy for you to keep it in mind. For now, the idea is to get the hang of the logic behind the thinking. Do not get too wrapped up in trying to remember the rules. They will become second nature soon enough. Moreover, I am purposely repeating the same thought in a variety of ways to try and embed the thought deep in one's psyche."

I asked an often enough raised question by many novices, "How long do you normally hold a stock? I find that buying is the easy part. Selling for capital preservation is easy as well since the sell-stop will take care of that. However, selling for profit is about the hardest thing in the markets. I have a hard time fixing the sell-for-profit decision. I end up selling too early or holding on too long. Is there a secret to finding the right timing in selling for profit just after the move ends but just before the opposing trend begins?"

Boyd gathered his thoughts for a few moments. Then he answered slowly, choosing his words carefully. I suspected that he wanted to ensure that there was no confusion on this rather complicated but simple reasoning. He said, "The problem comes about when the sell-for-profit is an instantaneous decision. In that respect, the problem is similar to an instantaneous decision made when one is buying a stock. Now that we are talking about this matter, any instantaneous decision is problematic. An instantaneous decision is an indication of a lack of discipline, a lack of respect for the market and a lack of knowledge. An instantaneous decision also is an indication of a lack of ability to follow the rules. If one catches himself or herself making an instantaneous decision, one must try and stop the action and do nothing. In most cases, instantaneous decisions are wrong decisions. It is not a reasoned, thought out and considered decision and consequently has bad odds of showing a winning move."

"Selling for profit must accomplish many results simultaneously. To sell for profits, one must sell when the up trend has ended and before the down trend has begun. To come to that tipping point where incremental gains have large odds of losses is an art that can be only developed after some years of practice. We discussed the simplest way to sell for profit when we talked about a trailing stop yesterday. In my opinion, it still is the best way to deal with the sell-for-profit dilemma."

## Twelfth rule of Speculation: Stocks within 15-20% of their all time prior high prices should be the ones to watch.

We know that stocks that are moving up in price are the only ones we want to buy. Stocks that are moving up in price show many of the winning characteristics including a clearly visible up trend. During the up trend, they will correct and base or consolidate for some periods of time. It is during these periods that we should start watching them for unusual volume activity. As soon as such stocks break out to new highs from the basing or the consolidating phase, we should be looking to buy them. To get such stocks on our watch list, we should pay attention to only those that are within 15-20% of their prior highs. This will help cut down on the number of stocks to watch. We only need a handful of stocks to prove or disprove the market's strength. The top stocks from the best performing industry groups should be more than enough to give us an indication of the market's condition.

## Thirteenth Rule of Speculation: Do not watch your computer during the day for any real time data. Only day-traders watch the market minute by minute and second by second.

Some of the worst decisions novices make is when they place a spontaneous trade. A spontaneous trade is when they make an instantaneous decision on a buy or a sell. It comes about especially when there is news related activity in the market. The news may or may not relate to an earnings report or a stock split or FDA approval of a drug being made by a pharmaceutical company which may cause activity in the drug company's stock, etc. Basically one is watching the ticker symbol and its bid-ask spreads and trading on one's computer and a sudden burst of volume and price activity causes folks to make an instantaneous buy or sell decisions.

These bad decisions come about because one is watching the market and stocks second by second. As seducing as it may be, many a seasoned speculator will acknowledge that such activity and behavior is devastating to most accounts. The stock market uses news to shake-out and fake-out weak folks. The true move and the trend is well in place far in advance of the news. The stock has already moved in anticipation of the news. The news only confirms the prior move. So a news related trade is only for seasoned day-traders. The rest of us should not even be watching the ticker tape.

The buy decision should be arrived at after considerable deliberation. This decision comes about based completely on the rules of speculation. Once the buy decision has been made, a buy-stop is usually the best way to enter the market. If the buy-stop order gets triggered, then the sell decision is left to the sell-stops to trigger. As discussed before, upon a buy being triggered a simultaneous sell-stop for loss-protection is placed. As the stock moves up and starts to log higher highs and higher lows, the sell-stop is moved up along the trending move. At some point one of the stops will get hit. More often than not, the sell-stop will get hit when the easiest and the fastest move up is over. Then on, should the stock offer any moves up, it is usually fraught with choppiness, volatility, fake outs and shake-outs. The incremental additional gains is not worth the risk of giving back any of the hard earned gains.

### Fourteen Rule Of Speculation:  Do not listen to any human beings about the market's general condition.  Let the leading stocks and the leading indices dictate your actions.

Boyd used to say that the only consistent winner in the stock market was the market.  The market is never wrong.  Humans are almost always wrong.  Humans are wrong about the direction or are wrong about the timing.  Either way, most humans have a very little shot at making big gains in the market.  Each one of us has our own bias and agenda in the market.

When a human opinion in elicited, the response is based strongly on one's own bias.  If the respondent is long the market, it is unlikely he will be bearish.  Similarly if the respondent is short the market, it is unlikely that he will be bullish.  Whatever is the respondent's own position in the market will be the determinant in his view expressed about the market.

Boyd used to say that CNBC and Bloomberg and other TV outlets should be turned off forever and never ever be turned on by the speculator.  In this day and age, stock market news and data is disbursed by all media at all times of the day.  It is hard to keep away from the deluge of information.  But a true speculator will remember at all times to listen to and pay attention to only the leading stocks and the leading indices.  The true message is there.  Not within any human.  It does not matter who the human being is.  Boyd used to say, "I have known some very successful speculators who stopped being so successful once they started babbling their view to the media.  The media has a way of making one feel more important than one is and suddenly a disciplined speculator becomes prey to the human element of self-importance and starts indicating what he wishes the market would do rather than maintaining the cold distance and seeing what the market is actually doing."

Perhaps it was this discipline that kept Boyd out of the limelight.  He shunned any attention from the market insiders and participants.  As I said before, very few knew him and fewer knew of him.  He would say when asked about his take on the market, "Do not listen to what I say as what I say may be biased and offered to you from my eyes. You should look at the market from your own eyes and no one else's. However, since you asked, I can only answer one of two ways…either the market is tradable or it is not tradable. In a tradable market, it is possible to make tradable gains and in an untradable market no gains can be made. This one now is an untradable market. It is better not to buy anything right now."

## Fifteenth Rule of Speculation: Stocks will do what they want to do. No one person can stop a stock from moving in one direction or another.

At first glance this rule may sound simplistic. But the idea is to imprint in the speculator's mind that stocks will almost never follow a script. In other words, though conditions may indicate a bull trend and leading stocks may start to be working, a change of trend can happen at any time. A stock may hit its stop and trigger its sell any time. A stock clearly in a strong up trend may reverse at any time. In the stock market anything can happen at any time. No matter how sure of an impending move a speculator is, he could be wrong in his view of the true trend. On the other hand, the speculator could be completely right and may just plain fall victim to a serious or a severe shake-out. One could be right on all accounts and still get taken out of a big mover due to a severe shakeout. These things happen to the best of us. The market is a tricky entity and the challenges are plentiful.

## Sixteenth Rule of Speculation: Decision making should be simple. Life is already pretty complicated. No need to add to this with burdens of heavy decision making in stock trading.

The harder we dig, the deeper the hole. Boyd used say that in the thirst for superior research and the urgency to "get there first," most humans will see things that are not there. The inbuilt bias and the wish that they have discovered a true untapped gem of a stock before the crowd will allow humans to make stupid mistakes. The secret is not to get in before a move has begun because the move may never begin. Or worse still, the move may start but head in the wrong direction. The true speculator understands that it is always best to get in once the move is in full swing. To wait for the move to be in full swing requires an 'unlearning' of all the typical life lessons we have learned in our lives. We have been brain washed and it has been drilled into us that the "early bird gets the worm." This makes humans believe that a superior research and knowledge of a stock and its products will help them reap rewards when the stock takes off. Whereas a true speculator will wait to confirm that the stock is indeed taking off before making commitments.

It is hard to unlearn the life lessons and then learn new lessons which look contrary to the life lessons we bring with us in to the market place.

### Seventeenth rule of Speculation: The market's sole job is to confuse us and fool us. Always look for confirming signs. Be in a hurry to sell a loss and reluctant to sell a profit. Let your stops make the decisions for you.

We have all heard about the $10,000 invested in the Wal-marts and the Ciscos and the Microsofts of this world at their IPO inception that turned into millions and millions of dollars. The odds of someone buying and holding through ups and downs through decades on the rare mover is very low indeed. For example, assume you bought $10,000 worth of Cisco at its inception. Let us assume some time into your buy the account has gone up to $150,000. The temptation to sell out at this level is immense. It becomes even more of a temptation to sell out if your $150,000 starts to drop in value. Let us say the $150,000 drops to $125,000 and then to $90,000...just how many would sit through such reactions? Nobody will ever talk to us about these reactions because the machinery does not want us to be "realistic." The machinery wants us to focus on the "buy and hold" riches that are there in the market. If "buy and hold" was such a great idea no one would have suffered losses during the 2000-2003 bear cycle. Just ask the holders of Global Crossing,

Worldcom, etc. who held to their $50 stocks all the way down to where the stocks were worth pennies.

**Eighteenth Rule of Speculation: Breakaways are solid bets. In an up trending market breakaways that meet most of the true breakaway criteria usually indicate the beginning of a true up trending move.**

Breakaway gaps were discussed in a prior lesson. Breakaways are true indicators of a beginning of a serious move. Depending upon the stage of the market cycle and where in the particular stock's cycle we are, the breakaway has good odds of a good run. The main challenge on a true breakaway is an effective way to trade successfully through the best portion of the breakaway's move.

**Nineteenth Rule of Speculation: Breakout day volume should explode. If a speculator's intention is to look for just a handful of potential trades for any given year, he should demand at least the stock's daily average volume of shares to be traded within the first hour of the trading session.**

Boyd had discussed the true meaning of a break out stock during an earlier breakfast. We know that the machinery will define breakouts as a move from one trading range to another without any regard to the true firm and confirmed trend of the stock or the market. A true breakout, by our definition, is a stock that has been basing for long periods of time (ranging from months to years). After this basing period, the stock begins a clearly visible strong up trend into all time new price highs on confirming volume strength. After such a prior up trend has been established, the stock then bases or rests for some period of time (ranging from weeks to months). After the rest is over, the stock breaks out to the upside into new all time price high area, yet again with confirming volume strength. This is our true breakout.

If we are the kinds of speculators who wish to trade only the best stocks from the best groups at the right time, then we will demand that within our watch list we pay attention only to the top 2 or 3 stocks at all times. And should one of these top 2 or 3 stocks break out on volume that meets our threshold level, then it becomes a buy at break out.

If a stock trades 500,000 shares on an average day, then to meet our threshold of a buy, it must trade 500,000 shares within the first hour of trade. First hour of trade, as we know, is from 9:30 a.m. to 10:30 a.m. EST.

## Twentieth Rule of Speculation:  Keep a written journal of each and every trade.  Learn from your mistakes.

A true speculator will enter each trade with a great amount of deliberation. He will check off his list of rules before coming to a conclusion that a commitment in the market place is indicated. And even when such an indication is given by the rules, he only enters with test-buys or small amounts to test the waters and see if his take on the market and the stock is correct.

If his test buy is proven to be correct, then he will take the second step of additional buys. Each step forward is dictated by the outcome of the prior step. In other words, he takes one step at a time and moves forward step by step. To indoctrinate the discipline firmly in his mind and in his psyche, he would develop the all important habit of writing down each and every trade he executes.

The reason for the buy, the amount bought, the price and the date the buy was triggered are all jotted down in a trade journal. The sell stops are moved right along the trending move. These sell-stops are also jotted down along with the reasons for moving the sell-stops up. At some point one of the sell-stops gets triggered and the position is sold out for profit. This sell-date, sell-price and the amount gained is also jotted down.

An example of a trade journal is shown in Table 1. This is a reproduction of Boyd's trade journal as he had offered to me on his trades of Taser International. I had covered his trades on Taser, where he had made an incredible profit of about $1.8 million on about $250,000 invested within six months, in my first book, "The Perfect Stock."

| Date | Action | Ticker | Quantity | Price | Reason for the action taken |
|------|--------|--------|----------|-------|------------------------------|
| 10/03/03 | Buy | TASR | 1500 | $32.68 GTC | Breakout to all time new highs after the 9/17 breakout on highest volume in 52 weeks which was confirmed by weekly charts |
| 10/03/03 | Sell-stop | TASR | 1500 | $29.68 GTC | Standard 10% stop-loss rule as loss-protection or capital preservation |
| 11/20/03 | Buy | TASR | 2800 | $69.75 GTC | Pyramid buy as stock breaks out to new highs after weeks of consolidation |
| 11/20/03 | Sell-stop | TASR | 4300 | $56.84 GTC | Standard 10% below the last buy loss cutting rule. Plus also ensures no loss taken on the over-all trade. |
| 01/09/04 | Buy | TASR | 2150 | $93.75 | Margin pyramid buy as stock breaks out to new highs after weeks of consolidation |
| 01/09/04 | Sell-stop | TASR | 6450 | $85.22 GTC | Standard 10% below last buy stop loss rule. Plus also ensures no loss taken on the over-all trade |

| 02/27/04 | Sell-stop | TASR | 6450 | $142.50 GTC | Stop placed a little below last week's low as reaction last week was severe on heavy volume |
| 03/26/04 | Sell-stop | TASR | 6450 | $173 GTC | Stop placed a little below last week's low |
| 04/02/04 | Sell-stop | TASR | 6450 | $209 GTC | Stop placed a little below last week's low |
| 04/09/04 | Sell-stop | TASR | 6450 | $232 GTC | Stop placed a little below last week's low |
| 04/16/04 | Sell-stop | TASR | 6450 | $277 GTC | Stop placed a little below last week's low |
| 04/19/04 | Sell at the market | TASR | 6450 | $351 | Sell out near the end of the trading day as the stock shows an exhaust top |

Table 1. Boyd's Taser trading records

Boyd used to say, "The art of learning through writing is lost. In this day and age where nobody writes in long hand anymore, the true art of writing is being lost. In the old age I learned my lessons in school by writing. The principles of learning since the early ages has been tied to the art of writing. When you write something down often enough, it is hard to forget. And we humans forget everything. To overcome this human deficiency, I learned long ago to write down all my trades. This way, I can go back to my winning trades and see what I did right. Similarly, I can go back to my losing trades and see where I made mistakes. The winning and losing trades may not repeat as an exact replica in the future, but there will be enough similarities for me to take advantage of based on my past experiences. This is an invaluable tool. However, like everything else in successful speculation, this requires discipline. And discipline, my friend, only comes about after large losses."

## Summary:

Stocks within 15-20% of their all time prior high prices should be the ones to watch. Do not watch your computer during the day for any real time data. Only day-traders watch the market minute by minute and second by second. Do not listen to any human beings about the market's general condition. Let the leading stocks and the leading indices dictate your actions. Stocks will do what they want to do. No one person can stop a stock from moving in one direction or another. Decision making should be simple. Life is already pretty complicated. No need to add to this with burdens of heavy decision making in stock trading. The market's sole job is to confuse us and fool us. Always look for confirming signs. Be in a hurry to sell a loss and reluctant to sell a profit. Let your stops make the decisions for you. Breakaways are solid bets. In an up trending market breakaways that meet most of the true breakaway criteria usually indicate the beginning of a true up trending move. Breakout day volume should explode. If a speculator's intention is to look for just a handful of potential trades for any given year, he should demand at least the stock's daily average volume of shares to be traded within the first hour of the trading session. Keep a written journal of each and every trade. Learn from your mistakes.

# CHAPTER 14
## BRUSHING UP THE BASICS

As I was nearing the end of the lessons and the breakfast get-togethers with Boyd, I was well aware that my style of writing was going to be far different from that of Boyd's. I was also quite aware that I had the tendency to assume that my readers were in sync with my thinking. This tended to make my writing some what herky-jerky to those that could not follow my train of thought.

To overcome this short-coming, I figured I probably should repeat some of the basics in various different forms and this would facilitate the reader in grasping the basics in many forms. I had a self-interest here. I knew if I wrote down the lessons, I would learn much for myself. Just as Boyd had commented on the fact that we should write to learn, I was getting the hang of the market more and more by my own writing down the stuff I knew and the stuff Boyd knew. The more I wrote, the more it became clearer.

It was then that I realized the value in Boyd's rule that one should write down all the trades one executes. And that such writings should include complete details of the reasons, amounts, gains/losses, etc. There was no substitute for on-the-job training. Practice makes perfect and one learns through doing.

It was clear to me that the pure principles of speculation, as laid out by Boyd, were learned by me and many others through actual experience in the market place. It was also obvious to me that very few would be able to grasp the importance of each and every rule unless the individual speculator experiences the losses himself or herself. It is the losses that teach the true lessons. The rules only becomes evident after sustained and serious losses.

As a result, I had to some how try and convince the novices that it is always best to start with a minimal amount of funds before embarking upon large commitments. The learning curve is long and slow and will offer many losses. To get through the years and the cycles of actual learning requires patience. It also requires one to be able to commit to only a small amount into the market in order to learn before the proper best odds trades can be placed. One needs to learn to place the best odds trades before placing large funds. It is no use placing large funds in low odds trades. That only guarantees losses of significant proportions sooner or later.

As most of us come in to the market with only a limited amount of funds, we have to learn without losing a significant amount of our funds. Learning takes time and it takes losses. We are not like the big funds who have a large pool of cash. They have the ability to withstand large losses and still come back during a serious bull trend. However, we have to make sure that the funds we have are in tact and we do not lose them trying to squeeze crumbs in a lousy market. And then, in turn, have nothing left when a true bull trend begins.

Among the many common mistakes most novices will make are over-trading and being arrogant. These two weaknesses alone can cut deep and hard quickly. In good markets, the odds of making winning trades may get above 50%. However, in lousy markets it should not be unreasonable to expect the odds of winning trades to drop off to well below 20%. Which means, perhaps one in five trades will be a winning trade in lousy conditions. In addition, the winning trade will prove to be very hard to trade effectively as it will offer very many shakeouts and fake-outs and it would be almost impossible to hold the stock without getting stopped out. Since the big money is only made when one can sit with a stock for 4-6-8 month periods, what good are winning stocks if they refuse to allow us to hold them for the intermediate time frame? That means, even if one was lucky enough or savvy enough to grab a winning trade in lousy conditions, odds are high that no serious gains can be made. As a result, despite winning once out of five times, the loss column keeps growing. It is far better to stay put in cash and not trade when odds are bad. However, this is a lesson that one learns after years of experience and huge losses.

In my earlier book, "The Perfect Stock," I had discussed the process of learning in the stock market to the process of getting through puberty. Almost all of us remember, if we try hard enough, the days long gone by when we were going through adolescence and the wisdom offered by our parents. Hardly anyone of us, at that moment in time now long gone, ever thought our parents to be wise. We all thought, "Times are different now. What do they know?" Well, it is no different in the learning process in the stock market. As novices, all of us go through periods where we think we know everything, that the market can be handily beaten, that the bull never dies, the bear never comes, that those olden days are long gone and many other typical teenager-type statements are bandied about. Welcome to adulthood. Nobody can escape the cycles. It is only after many years of hardship and difficulty in making in-roads in the market, we learn. Just like the lessons we learn in adulthood that what our parents told us was true and indeed they knew a little something about life when we were carefree teenagers. When we try to impart similar lessons to our offspring, it should not be surprising that their reactions are no different than the ones we had when we were their age.

The market's lessons are the same. Humans just do not want to hear it or learn it. They want easy rides, free money and bargains galore. If only one put one's mind and hard-work into it, the rewards can be immense. But that takes time and patience. Not exactly a human forte.

## Summary:

Keep it short and simple (K.I.S.S). Simplest is always best.

# CHAPTER 15
## THE BASIC ROUTINE

During the waning days of my meetings with Boyd, I asked him to let me in on his typical routine when he approached the market. I took down notes hurriedly when he spoke that day. I wished to model my daily routine along the lines of his. As it turned out, I did not need to take too many notes as his routine was simple. Exactly the way he liked it.

That night I typed up the summary of the day's lessons. And it looked like this:

- Start off every weekend looking at weekly index charts on the DJIA, Nasdaq, S&P500 and the Transports. Pay particular attention to the price/volume action and verify if the indices are in a specific trend. If the trend is not clear or if the trend is downward, then buying stocks is not a good idea and it is better to wait for better days.
- If the trend is clear and it is upward, then it is time to be looking to buy test-case amounts into stocks that are showing a confirmed up trend.
- In order to see where the strength lies and which stocks are the right potentials, take a look at stocks making new 52-week highs. Check them out on their all time charts and verify if they show the right kind of price and volume action. If they show the right kind of price/volume action on their all time weekly and monthly charts, then jot them down on your list of stocks to watch.
- In addition to the stocks you have jotted down, look at the sister stocks of these "stock-to-watch." If any sister stocks confirm or show a similar action as the ones on

your "stocks to watch" list, then odds are better with these two stocks than any other.

- Check to see if any of your "stocks to watch" are making in-roads into or are near "all time high price." Those that are would make your true "short list of potential buys." Once you have this short list, then we must start looking at daily action. That means, after the market has closed, check for the stock's daily, weekly and monthly charts. Daily charts can be for the most recent one year. Weekly charts can also be for the most recent one, but no more than three years. Monthly charts are for all data. If what is seen is confirmed by all three charts - daily, weekly and monthly charts - then what we see is likely happening. In other words, we are not seeing something that is not happening. Once we identify such stocks, we then have to fix the exact entry price.
- Keep track every weekend on weekly charts the movements as shown by the leading indices.
- Once an entry into an individual stock has been made, an immediate corresponding sell-stop needs to be placed. The sell-stop can only be moved up once the stock proves to be a 20/4 type mover. Should the stock make a 20/4 type move, the sell-stop is then move to a little above one's buy price so that no loss is taken on a stock that proved to be a 20/4 type mover. Thereafter, the sell-stop once placed, cannot be changed until a new clearly visible and higher priced sell-stop comes about.
- If possible, move stops solely based on weekly charts.
- During the week, do not to watch any intra-day stock movements.
- Turn off the TV (CNBC and Bloomberg and others), cancel your subscriptions to all the major business, investment and stock market newspapers and magazines. The more well-known the media outlet, the worse the market timing and direction offered. To be successful in the market, the speculator has to be right about the market's direction and he has to be right about his timing of the move. In addition, a successful speculator has to be able to "think and act" in a vacuum. In other words,

at times when the market looks the best, he has to sell out and when the market looks the worst he has to buy. And at other times, even if the market looks good he cannot buy and even if the market looks terrible he cannot sell. How the market looks to the public or the media should never come into the equation of how the speculator sees the market and how he acts on what he sees.

## Summary:

Develop and follow your own daily and weekly routine. There is no substitute for a routine in implementing one's rules of successful speculation.

## CHAPTER 16
## COMMIT AFTER THE MOVE STARTS

It is unbelievable how ingrained in our minds is the thought that we must catch the move before it starts. Perhaps it comes from our caveman mentality where the first one to catch the hunt ate. Or perhaps it is the lifelong lessons we learn from our childhood that life is a race and the faster we begin the race better the odds of us beating the rest of the crowd. Perhaps it is the lessons learned through the ages where the first one who dug up the gold was the first to win the treasure.

The mantra of "get in before the move starts" is such an integral part of our human psyche that the crowd is in a rush to pick the turning points in the market. The stampede is fueled by the insiders who will hype every rally as the beginning or a continuation of a bull market. Even the term "bull market" conjures up images of a charging bull heading straight on. The marketing machinery is in place and the hype is always moments away. Even during the deepest depths of a bear market, the marketing machinery is churning out new prospects and new "have to buy" lists to peddle to the public.

Boyd used to say that most of the money is lost during the "chasing the false rallies" phase of a bear market. A classic one liner that Boyd would use was, "Do not buy until the move is definitely on." Just how many of us can wait out the false rallies? The need to not miss out on anything is so strong and so powerful, that even the best of us have to surround ourselves with a set of rigid rules to avoid the traps.

It is always better to be late than early in the stock market. In other words, never be early to the party. There is no guarantee that every party will be a success. Better to wait and confirm that a good looking party is on before arriving to the party. It is always better to get in after the move has started than before a move has started. The questions one must bear in mind are:

- If I get in before a move, what guarantee do I have that a move will occur?
- Even if the move should occur, what guarantee is there that the move will be in my direction?
- How long do I have to wait before the move actually occurs?

The speculator's mentality of waiting to confirm that a move is definitely on before making commitments works in all endeavors of life and not just in the search for stock market riches. It is the same in real estate. It makes no sense to buy into a real estate property before a move has started. One could be sitting holding on to a useless piece of property for one's entire life. On the other hand, once a serious move has begun, many a real estate speculative moves have panned out well for the smart speculator who waited until the move was certainly on.

## Summary:

Make no commitments until a serious move has been confirmed to be definitely on.

# CHAPTER 17
## THE EXPERIENCED LOSER OR THE EXPERIENCED WINNER

One learns by doing. We learn to crawl by actually crawling. We learn to walk by actually walking ourselves. We learn to run and swim by actually running and swimming ourselves. Yes, during the process of learning to crawl, walk and run, we fall, get hurt, slow down, stumble and scratch ourselves. And during the process of learning to swim we drink tons of dirty water, our eyes hurt, our ears hurt. However, once the learning process is done, we know the pitfalls to avoid. We might still fall once in a while, however, we hardly ever get seriously hurt.

It is no different in the stock market. The learning process is slow and long and painful. If one throws in the towel, one has no shot at learning the lessons of successful speculation.

Most folks want easy direct answers for making it in the markets. When folks like Boyd Hunt comply and offer truly tested lessons, the students do not want to listen. The lessons, as offered by folks like Boyd, are too cumbersome, old-fashioned, slow to show gains, require long periods of thinking, learning and understanding the markets. It requires unlearning the lessons that were learned in our other endeavors in life. The biggest lessons relate to self-discipline and conquering the human element.

Boyd would say that the market place is filled with experienced folks. However, most are experienced losers since over any ten-year cycle most folks will be lucky to come out even. The experienced winners are few and far between and usually the silent ones. The experienced winner, by logic, has to be silent because he has to be bearish when the entire world is bullish. To speak one's mind when the crowd is bullish is asking to be ostracized and we are all social animals. To be ostracized is not desired by any one of us and the experience is not pleasant.

It is someone like Boyd, who by nature is distant and detached, that can be successful as folks like him do not have any need to be socializing. Boyd had spent years getting beaten up by the market. He had learned the lessons harshly. There was no need in him to prove his abilities to anyone. His abilities were known to him and him alone and to him that was all that mattered. He had no need to advertise his wins or his right market calls. He had nothing to prove to anyone. To him, the proof of his abilities was in the value of his trading account. That trading account had a value which had more than a handful of zeroes beside it.

Some years ago when Boyd had decided to close his stock service, I had asked him why he was taking that step. After all, his picks were great and his market timing was better than anyone else's that I knew. And I knew quite a few successful operators in the market. His reply was, "I do not have in me to try and soothe every reader's human needs. People cannot wait to win. I was getting tired of the mind games people played. When the market was turning and I was telling my readers to be wary, they wanted to be bullish and informed me that the best bull market in decades was in the offing. Once I was proven right in a matter of weeks or months, many readers would feel as if I was insulting their intelligence by my writing where I would point out that the signs I saw were clearly being played out."

He continued, "The people who cannot wait out the bad periods cannot wait with stocks in good times. Whether the conditions are good, bad or indifferent, waiting is the key to success. Nobody wants to wait. In bad times, I would suggest waiting in cash. Nobody wanted to wait out the bad times. They would either trade their way in and out of the market into a deep hole or cancel out their subscriptions. Once the good times came about, those that would trade their way in and out of the market would make a few points. Some of the others would sell out of big winners early on and miss out the true move. Many would come into the market very late. In all these cases, the lack of ability to sit tight and wait was the key reason for missing the big and true moves in the market."

"The market is filled with risk. I cannot justify losing 10% to make 10%. If I am going to be involved with the market, it better offer me some pretty good odds of doubling my money. Otherwise, the risk is not worth the involvement. If many truly winning stocks are not being offered, the market has no use for me."

"When I decided to stop my service, I received discreet emails and calls from a handful of readers who wished me to continue with the work. I ended up servicing only these readers with my commentary. These readers have stuck with me now for many decades and I have a hard time taking leave from them."

"I have informed them in my last column that I am handing over the reigns to you and that you are about as good as they come. They respect my ability to recognize a good operator and I have full confidence that you will serve them well and they will treat you well in turn."

"I never saw the need to expand my readership. I liked my life kept simple. I was not much into trying to be a widely read writer. I would encourage you to keep it that way. There is no need for the extra headaches that come with a large subscriber base. It becomes easy to lose focus and get too involved in trying to please everybody. The goal of the writer of these kinds of columns is to interpret the market correctly, pick the right stocks at the right time and then to trade them effectively. As long as you keep your eyes on the goal, you will be alright."

I realized that Boyd had already given the reigns to me. He said, "I suggest you get started immediately. I am writing my last column this weekend and I will bid good-bye to my readers. I am quite happy and content with my selection of a successor. I appreciate your accepting the challenge. I can assure you that you will learn much from the readers and I am sure they will learn much from you and your fresh perspective."

That night as I started putting all of my notes from Boyd's lessons in a book form, I felt lonely as I could feel the huge loss of a giant of a man and dear friend. I wondered, just to whom would I now turn to in times of confusion in the market. Then I realized that Boyd had given me everything I needed to navigate through the dangerous waters when he had said, "Listen to the market and the leading stocks. They will hardly ever steer you wrong. Never listen to humans as humans are almost always wrong. The market is the only one who is never wrong."

I felt confident. I knew that the market was my friend and my only true guide. Apart from the market and the leading stocks, I had no reason to depend or rely upon anyone or anything else. Boyd had made the market a good friend of mine. As was his style, in an unassuming and discreet fashion, Boyd had left behind a great gift to me. I was very fortunate and my hope was to share this fortune with those who were willing to put the time, effort and hard-work in making the market their friend.

## Summary:

The market is a speculator's only true friend as the market will never steer a speculator wrong.

# APPENDIX 1
## THE RULES OF SPECULATION

1. First, do no harm.

2. Check off your check-list before buying: ( ) Is the general market in a confirmed up trend? ( ) Do I see any 20/4 type stock movements? ( ) Do I see price/volume action that confirms everything I see?

3. If I cannot make money on test-buys, I cannot make money on large funds.

4. Always use a stop-loss in place to protect the account from oneself.

5. The trend is your friend and move your stops along the trending move.

6. I must start making gains on my positions from Day One and within four weeks, the stock must have made at least a 20% or more move from the buy price to its new high prices. The 20/4 type stocks should continue to be in an up trend where they keep logging higher highs and higher lows.

7. Do not buy a second stock and do not make a pyramid buy on the first stock unless the first buy has made a gain.

8. Pyramid only when odds are working in your favor and make sure that the pyramid buy will never result in a loss on the over-all trade.

9. If many leading 20/4 type stocks start hitting their stops, the market maybe showing signs of danger.

10. Do not look to make any gains in bad markets. It is far better to stay out of bad markets where odds of wins are against us, rather than trying to swim against the tide.

11. If the best stocks are not moving up in price, the market has no chance of offering good odds of wins. If the best stocks are moving up, no other reason is needed to be buying and if the best stocks are not moving up in price, no other reason is needed to avoid buying.

12. Stocks that are within 15-20% of their all time prior price highs should be the ones to watch.

13. Do not watch your computer during market hours for real time data. Only day-traders watch the market minute by minute and second by second.

14. Do not listen to any human beings about the market's general conditions. Let the leading stocks and the leading indices dictate your actions.

15. Stocks will do what they want to do. No one person can stop a stock from moving in one direction or another.

16. Decision making should be simple. Life is already pretty complicated. No need to add to this with the burdens of heavy decision making in stock trading.

17. The market's sole job is to confuse us and fool us. Always look for confirming signs. Be in a hurry to sell a loss and reluctant to sell a profit. Let your stops make your decisions for you.

18. Breakaways are solid bets. In an up trending market, breakaways that meet most of the true breakaway criteria usually indicate the beginning of a true up trending move.

19. Breakout day volume should explode.    If a speculator's intention is to look for just a handful of potential trades for any given year, he should demand at least the stock's daily average volume of shares to be traded within the first hour of the trading session.

20. Keep a written journal of each and every trade.  Learn from your mistakes.  Your mistakes will teach you a lot about yourself. These lessons cannot be taught by anyone else.

# APPENDIX 2
## A PICTURE IS WORTH A THOUSAND WORDS

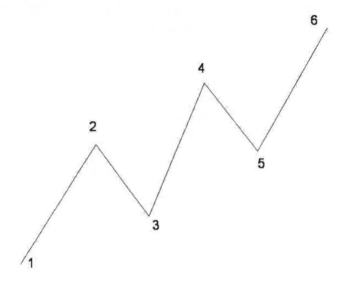

**Figure 1. A confirmed up trend**

1 = most recent low

2 = a near term high pegged by an up trending stock

3 = a reactionary low pegged in response to the high pegged at point 2

4 = new higher high above the prior high of point 2

5 = a reactionary low to the most recent high at point 4

6 = a new higher high

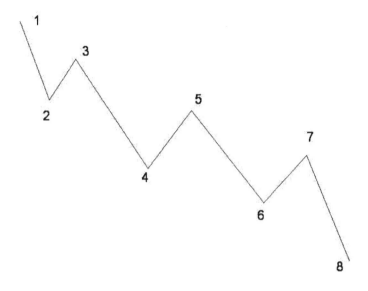

**Figure 2. A confirmed down trend**

1 = most recent high

2 = a near term term low is pegged by a down trending stock

3 = a reactionary high is pegged in response to the downward leg from point 1 to point 2

4 = a new lower low is pegged in continuation of the down trend

5 = a reactionary high is lower than the prior high at point 3

6 = a new lower low is pegged

7 = the reactionary high is yet again lower than the prior high at point 5

8 = continuation of the down trend

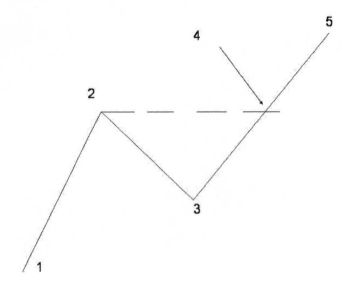

**Figure 3. A zig showing a potential up trend**

1 = prior up trend

2 = most recent high

3 = reactionary low to the most recent high

4 = as the high point pegged at point 2 is overcome and cleared, a potential new up trend may have begun

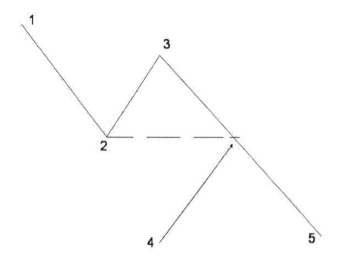

**Figure 4. A zag showing a potential down trend**

1 = prior down trend

2 = most recent low

3 = reactionary high to the most recent low

4 = as the new low point pegged at point 2 is penetrated to the down side, a potential new down trend may have begun

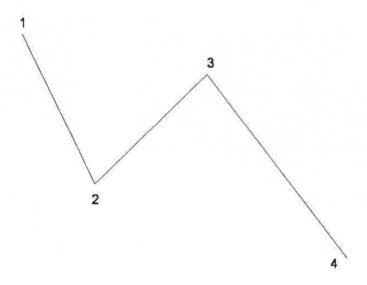

**Figure 5a. A down trending market**

1 = prior down trend

2 = most recent low

3 = reactionary high to the most recent low

4 = a new lower low

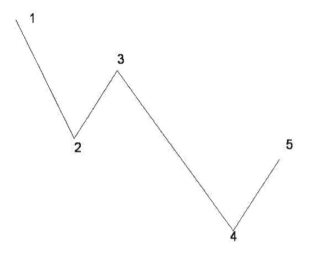

**Figure 5b. A potential changed trend may or may not be in the offing**

1 = prior down trend

2 = most recent low

3 = reactionary high to the most recent low

4 = a new lower low

5 = a rally off of point 4

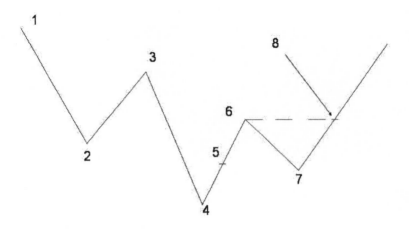

**Figure 5c. A change of trend**

1 = prior down trend

2 = most recent low

3 = reactionary high to the most recent low

4 = a new lower low

5 = a rally off the most recent low

6 = a high pegged during the most recent rally

7 = a downward reaction to the most recent rally, but this low is higher than the prior low at point 4

8 = as price reaches above point 6, the prior high, a new changed trend is indicated

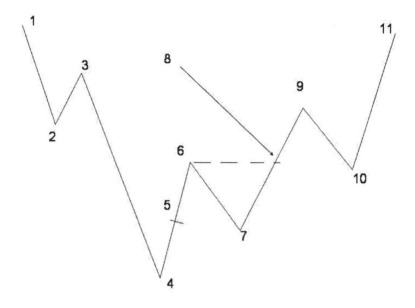

**Figure 5d. A change of trend is confirmed**

1 = prior down trend

2 = most recent low

3 = reactionary high to the most recent low

4 = a new lower low

5 = a rally off the most recent low

6 = a high pegged during the most recent rally

7 = a downward reaction to the most recent rally, but this low is higher than the prior low at point 4

8 = as price reaches above point 6, the prior high, a new changed trend is indicated

9 = a new higher high above the prior high at point 6 is pegged

10 = a higher low than the prior low at point 7 is pegged

11 = a new higher high continues the up trend

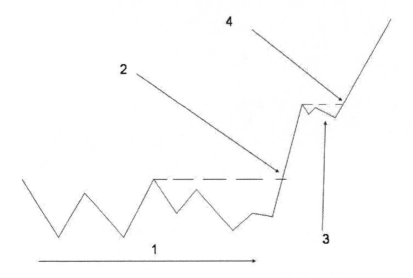

**Figure 6. A typical 20/4 type stock move**

1 = long basing phase lasting months and years

2 = all time new price highs are pegged

3 = consolidation or resting phase

4 = break out to new highs to proceed to make 20% or more move within four weeks from point 4 onward

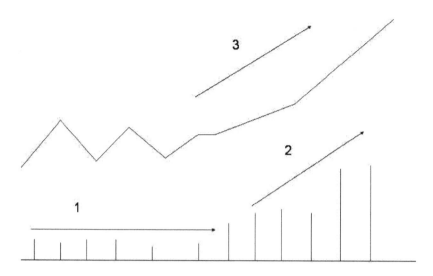

**Figure 7. An ideal price/volume action**

1 = long basing phase with quiet volume

2 = rising volume

3 = rising price accompanies rising volume

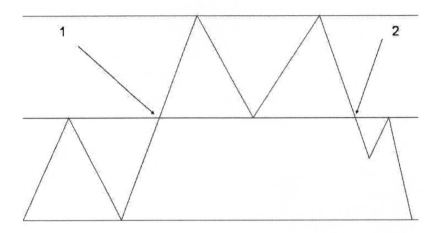

**Figure 8a. Any old breakout**

1 = a breakout from one price range to a higher price range

2 = return back to the original lower price range

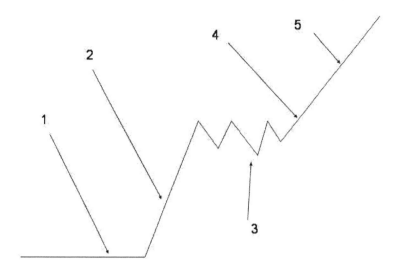

**Figure 8b. A true breakout**

1 = long sideways basing phase

2 = a strong up trend begun to make new price highs

3 = resting or consolidation phase

4 = breakout to new all time high price area

5 = continued up trend now resumed after the resting or consolidation phase

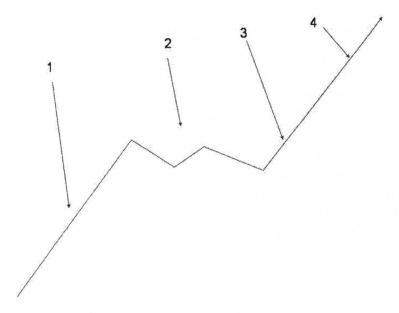

**Figure 8c. A close-up of a true breakout**

1 = a strong up trend begun to make new price highs

2 = resting or consolidation phase

3 = breakout to new all time high price area

4 = continued up trend now resumed after the resting or consolidation phase

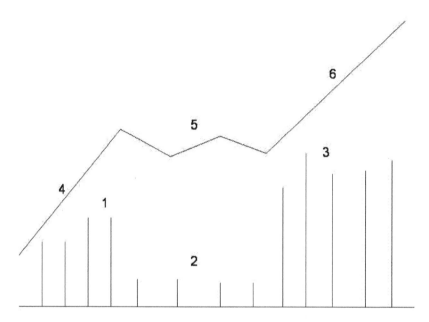

**Figure 9. A true breakout with solid price/volume action**

1 = rising volume during the prior up trend

2 = volume contraction during the resting or consolidating phase

3 = volume jumps to highest levels in the stock's all time history of trading volume

4 = prior up trend price area

5 = consolidation phase - the high price during this phase is a "ceiling" until the stock breaks above this "ceiling" price. Once it breaks above the "ceiling" price, then the "ceiling" becomes the "floor" price which is normally not penetrated to the down side again

6 = up trend resumes

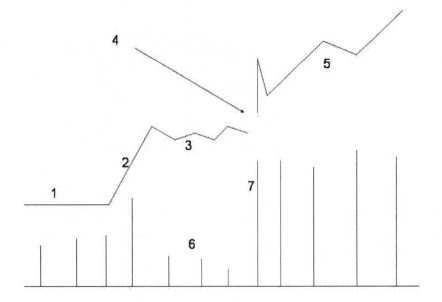

**Figure 10. A true breakaway**

1 = long sideways basing phase

2 = a strong up trend begun to make new price highs

3 = resting or consolidation phase

4 = breakaway gap

5 = continued up trend now resumed after the resting or consolidation phase

6 = dead volume during resting phase

7 = highest volume of trade shown in the stock's all time trading history

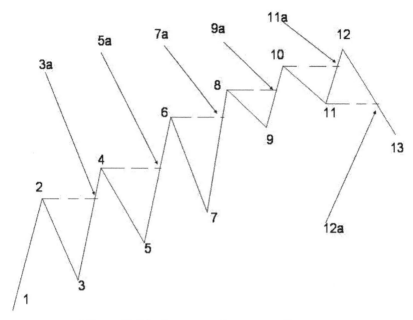

**Figure 11. Moving stops along a trending move**

Boyd said, "Assume you own a stock that is rising in price. I have drawn a sketch of such a stock. Let us say you bought the stock as it cleared the point 3a when it made new price highs. As soon as you get bought in at 3a, you would place a sell-stop at 10% below the price at 3a. Assume that the sell-stop price is not touched until the stock has logged a higher high and a higher low. This means the stock has to first log a high price at point 4. Then its reaction to this move up must be pegged, such as it is at a price at point 5. Note that the price at point 5 is higher than the price at point 3 - the stock's last low. Then the stock has to log a new higher high, such as it does at a price at point 6. Note that the price at point 6 is higher than its prior high price at point 4. During the course of the stock price's move from point 5 to a price at point 7, it passes through or pierces above the price at 5a which is essentially the same price as logged as a high at point 4. As soon as the stock pierces above this point 5a, the stock has now re-confirmed its up trend. It is at this point in time that the sell-stop is moved from the prior sell-stop to a little below the price at point 5."

"The sell-stop remains at a little below the price at point 5 until another round of higher highs and higher lows have been confirmed. This means the stock has to first log the high as indicated by the price at point 6. The stock must then react to this new high price at point 6. The reaction is shown to be pegging a low price at point 7. Then a new leg of upward move begins. During this new move up from the price at point 7 to the price at point 8, the stock must pierce or pass through the price high pegged at point 6. I have indicated this price to be a price at point 7a. As soon as the stock moves past this price at 7a, I then move my sell-stop from a little below the price at point 5 to a little below the price at point 7. The sell-stop placed now at a little below the price at point 7 is not moved until yet another complete round of higher highs and higher lows are pegged."

"On paper this seems quite simple and straight-forward enough. The biggest hurdle most novices face is that they pay attention to their account values and to their stock prices day in day out. When they see the stock has pegged a high at, for example, point 6 and then they see it react to the price at point 7, they start getting nervous. They feel that they are 'losing' their profit and the novice will sell out at the first hint of price weakness."

"The discipline to follow sell-stops along the trending move takes time to develop. Most folks get the hang of this discipline only after "missing out" on the big wins. It is only after many have let go of a true winner very early in the trend many many times, that many folks will get the hang of trading along the trend. Regrettably, many others will never get the grasp of the simplicity of the discipline. Like I said, time is relative. Four to eight months is not a long period of time in the stock market for people like me who have seen and experienced the gifts and the dangers of the market for decades. But for novices and many undisciplined professionals (who will not remain professionals for long), even 4-8 weeks seem like an eternity."

And he continued, "As the stock keeps making these higher highs and higher lows, the stops keep moving up along the trending move. At some point the upward price pressure will stop. And then the pressure starts to build to push the prices down. The turn comes with subtlety some times and at other times it comes with complete clarity. But the speculator who keeps his rules in place will keep moving his stops up. First the stop moves to a little below the price at point 9. Then to a little below the price at point 11. As the stock tops out for the intermediate or longer term and starts to head down, this stop will get hit and the stock is sold out. The speculator was thus able to ride with the stock from a price at point 3a to the price at point 11. That is a significant move and that is the true goal of a sharp speculator - to grab and ride the meaty or the significant part of a trending move."

## APPENDIX 3
## THE ONLY OTHER BOOKS A SPECULATOR NEEDS

1. "How I made $2 million in the stock market" by Nicolas Darvas

2. "How charts can help you in the stock market" by William Jiler

3. "The Perfect Stock" by Brad Koteshwar

All other lessons have to be learned by actual trade executions and experiencing a complete cycle consisting of an entire bull trend and an entire bear trend.

LAGO VISTA    10-15-22

9 780976 932406